Advanced Studies in Theoretical and Applied Econometrics
Volume 43

The titles published in this series are listed at the end of this volume.

Ivohasina Fizara Razafimahefa • Shigeyuki Hamori

International Competitiveness in Africa

Policy Implications in the Sub-Saharan Region

With 81 Figures and 30 Tables

Springer

Dr. Ivohasina Fizara Razafimahefa
Director of Economic Affairs Presidency
of the Republic of Madagascar
BP 955
Antananarivo 101
Madagascar
razafimahefa@hotmail.com

Prof. Shigeyuki Hamori
Kobe University
2-1, Rokkodai
Nada-Ku
Kobe 657-8501
Japan
hamori@econ.kobe-u.ac.jp

ISBN 978-3-642-08845-2 e-ISBN 978-3-540-68921-8

Springer is a part of Springer Science+Business Media
springer.com

Softcover reprint of the hardcover 1st edition 2007

Cover design: eStudio Calamar S.L., F. Steinen-Broo, Pau/Girona, Spain

To my late father and my mother,
To Hitoshi, Makoto and Naoko

Acknowledgements

We have benefited greatly from the support of many people in writing this volume. Special thanks are due to Martina Bihn for excellent editorial guidance. We also would like to thank our family members Rafalimanantsoa Aimée, Ando, Zo, Jadzia, Manoela, Thierry, Mamy, Miora, Anja, Hitoshi, Makoto and Naoko. Without their warm-hearted support, we could not have finished writing this volume. We are also very grateful to Jaime Marquez, Kazuhiro Igawa, and Masayuki Hara for their many helpful comments and suggestions. Our research is in part supported by a grant-in-aid from the Japan Society for the Promotion of Science.

Antananarivo, Madagascar — Ivohasina Fizara Razafimahefa
Kobe, Japan — Shigeyuki Hamori

Table of Contents

1 Introduction

The effects of international trade and foreign direct investment (FDI) on developing economies have always been controversial. From about the 1980s, however, the countries adopting open policies have tended to outperform those adopting closed policies. The former, essentially the economies of Asia and some countries of Latin America, have grown faster than the latter, the economies of sub-Saharan Africa. With the unstoppable spread of globalization and the supremacy of "open" policies over "closed" ones, the debate between "participating" and "not participating" in the world economy has been superseded by discussions on the best policy measures for expanding participation and enhancing the accrued welfare gains. The countries of sub-Saharan Africa have no choice but to take part in international trade and investment. Policies to strengthen international competitiveness are almost unanimously considered crucial means towards those ends.

A key way of making a country more competitive is to strengthen its international competitiveness in trade and investment. Competitiveness in international trade is defined, in the present analysis, as the ability of a country to produce and sell goods in the international market at a lower price than competitor countries. Competitiveness in international investment, on the other hand, is understood as the ability of a country to attract large inflows of foreign investment. Given that competitors also strive to increase their abilities to sell goods and attract, the study takes a dynamic approach, as opposed to a static approach, to comparative advantage.

This book examines two policies frequently used to enhance international competitiveness: the exchange rate policy and productivity policy. We explore the effectiveness of these policies in raising international competitiveness as assessed through two channels, namely, trade competitiveness and FDI competitiveness.

The book is structured as follows. Chapters 2 and 3 empirically analyze the trade-FDI and growth relationship in the countries of sub-Saharan Africa. The development of the new growth theory has led to a wide recognition of the potential power of international trade and FDI in enhancing growth. The analysis in Chap. 2 focuses on the relationship between international trade and economic growth. The analysis in Chap. 3

focuses on the relationship between FDI and economic growth. We use the standard time series technique, i.e. variance decomposition, to examine the problems in these chapters.

Chapters 4 and 5 examine policy measures with the potential to enhance trade by strengthening trade competitiveness. We focus specifically on exchange rate and productivity policies, delving into the effectiveness of each. The depreciation of a local currency can be expected to instantly lower the prices of a country's exports in foreign currency and thereby boost exports. At the same time, however, the depreciation might exert upward pressure on domestic inflation. If the export prices in a local currency rise as a result of this, the inflation might offset the expected effects of the exchange rate policy. In Chap. 4 we empirically investigate the exchange rate and inflation pass-through mechanism. Three techniques are applied in our investigation: a VAR (vector autoregression) or VEC (vector error correction)-based Granger causality test, an LA (lag augmented)-VAR-based causality test, and a CCF (cross correlation function)-approach-based causality test. Both causalities are tested, in mean and in variance. To directly inspect and compare the effectiveness of exchange rate policy and productivity policy in bringing about stronger trade competitiveness, Chap. 5 uses the "bounds" cointegration test to investigate how export prices relate to exchange rates and productivity over the long run.

Chapter 6 explores FDI competitiveness, or the ability of a country to attract foreign investment. Factors determining the inflows of FDI are investigated in order to seek out areas where policy measures can be implemented to improve the attractiveness of a country for foreign investors. Specifically, we use a panel data analysis to identify determinants of FDI and empirically analyze how those determinants relate to FDI inflow.

Having confirmed the importance and supremacy of productivity policy over exchange rate policy in the earlier chapters of the book, we try to find direct policy measures to enhance total factor productivity in Chap. 7. We use six determinants for empirical analysis, i.e. human capital, reallocation of production factors from low- to high-productivity sectors, agglomeration, demographic age structure, infrastructure development, and black market premiums. A panel causality test is used to empirically investigate these factors.

Trade deficits pose difficulties for sub-Saharan African countries. As economies grow, their demand for foreign goods grows in parallel and world trade benefits as a whole. Without a stable balance between exports and imports, however, a newly emerging trade deficit will tend to expand. Chapter 8 uses panel cointegration techniques to empirically analyze the sustainability of trade accounts.

Changes in an exchange rate affect a trade balance by changing the terms of trade. According to the Marshall-Lerner condition, deterioration in the terms of trade will improve a country's trade balance if the sum of the country's price elasticity of demand for exports and imports is greater than one in absolute value. Chapter 9 uses heterogeneous panel cointegration techniques to empirically examine the relationship between trade balance and terms of trade in sub-Saharan African countries.

According to the purchasing power parity (PPP) theory, the long-run equilibrium exchange rate of two currencies is the rate that equalizes the purchasing powers of the currencies. Over the long term, the exchange rate between the currencies shifts in accordance with the relative purchasing power of each. The simplicity and intuitive appeal of PPP has attracted many researchers and prompted many analyses of the theory. Chapter 10 uses heterogeneous panel cointegration techniques to empirically analyze whether the PPP theory holds true in sub-Saharan African countries.

This book closes with the concluding remarks in Chap. 11.

We hope that this work sheds light on the development of the countries of sub-Saharan Africa.

2 Trade and Economic Growth

2.1 Introduction

The trade and growth nexus has been a topic of intense debate among researchers as well as policymakers. For the former, findings from theoretical models and empirical investigations have led to heterogeneous, even diverging conclusions. For the latter, various and dissimilar policies have been tested and implemented across countries and across time. This chapter empirically analyzes the relationship between the foreign trade (openness) and economic growth for sub-Saharan African countries (Fig. 2.1).

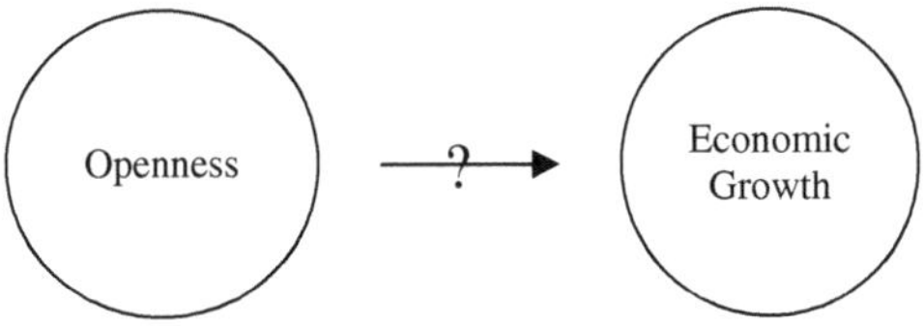

Fig. 2.1. Openness and economic growth

2.2 Literature Review

The literature on the trade and growth relationship can be classified into two groups: (i) studies that put forward the beneficial effects of trade on growth, what we qualify as "Pro's," and (ii) studies that emphasize either non-existent or adverse effects of trade on growth, what we call "Con's."

2.2.1 Pro's

In theoretical development, trade was portrayed as an important engine of growth from the time of Adam Smith up to the time of Ricardo and Solow. Trade leads to a better allocation of resources and allows a higher level of income. In the theoretical neoclassical growth model pioneered by Solow (1956), trade policy affects the allocation of resources between sectors along the transitional path as an economy converges towards its steady state. Trade thus influences the steady state level of savings and capital accumulation. After reaching the steady state, however, trade no longer affects the equilibrium growth of an economy, a process solely determined by an exogenous factor – technological progress.

The growth effects of trade openness are made more explicit by the use of the new growth theory led by Romer (1986) and Lucas (1988). Within this framework, Grossman and Helpman (1991) establish that openness enhances economic growth through the following channels. Trade enlarges the available variety of intermediate goods and capital equipment, which can expand the productivity of the country's other resources. Trade permits developing countries to access the improved technology in developed countries, in the form of embodied capital goods. Trade makes it possible to intensify capacity utilization, a process that increases products produced and consumed. Openness offers a larger market for domestic producers, allowing them to operate at a minimum required scale and to reap benefits from increasing returns to scale.

Many empirical studies have assessed the positive effect of trade on growth. Krueger (1978) uses data from individual country studies to test two hypotheses: (1): more liberalized regimes result in higher rates of growth of exports; and (2) a more liberalized trade sector has a positive effect on aggregate growth. In the latter case, Krueger argues that there are two channels through which openness positively affects growth. First, there are direct effects that operate via dynamic advantages, including higher capacity utilization and more efficient investment projects. Second, there are indirect effects that work through exports: more open economies have faster growth of exports and these, in turn, result in faster economic growth.

Feder (1982) discovers, from a cross-sectional analysis of 31 semi-industrialized countries, that exports have positive externality effects on economic growth. Esfahani (1991) extends Feder's work by introducing the idea that apart from the externality effects, the contribution of exports to growth appears more substantial through its effect of reducing import shortages. Esfahani tests the robustness of his findings by running a cross-sectional analysis of a set of semi-industrialized countries. He concludes that the significant impact of exports on growth is the alleviation of scarcity of imports faced by those countries. When the second channel is taken into account, the coefficient of the externality effects drops rather remarkably.

Coe, Helpman and Hoffmaister (1997) show that trade allows developing countries to benefit from research conducted in developed countries. Imports of a larger variety of intermediate and capital goods, which incorporate the outcome of research led in the developed trading partners, can increase the productivity of the developing economy. From a cross-sectional study of 77 developing countries, the work shows that R&D spillovers through trade are transmitted from 22 industrial countries to the former group.

Frankel and Romer (1996) address the controversy related to the endogeneity between trade variables and growth by introducing geographic factors to derive instrumental variables. They argue that those factors substantially determine conditions of trade and are unlikely to be directly correlated to growth. They conclude that trade has a significant positive effect on growth, and that the results from ordinary least squares underestimate that effect.

Edwards (1998) uses a data set of 93 countries to test the robustness of the impact of trade on growth by introducing nine measures of openness, first alternatively and then simultaneously. He concludes that each proxy for openness is correlated positively with economic growth and that the composite index from those proxies also enters with a positive coefficient in the growth regression.

Likewise, Wacziarg (2001) suggests a composite index of the usual measures. He studies the trade and growth relationship in a set of 57 countries. To deal with the direction of causality problem, he estimates the effects of the new openness indicator on six principal sources of economic growth: macroeconomic policy, government size, price distortion, factor accumulation, technology transfer, and foreign direct investment. He concludes that, depending on the specification, between 46% and 63% of the impact of trade openness on growth occurs through the accumulation of physical capital. He also argues that the analysis thoroughly captures the impact of trade on growth.

Most studies on the trade and growth relationship have employed the cross sectional approach. This approach has two main drawbacks, however. First, as pointed out by Harrison (1996), long-run averages are unsatisfactory measures of openness because they do not reflect the significant fluctuations in trade policy over time. Second, according to Jin (2000), cross-sectional analysis cannot distinguish the specific characteristics of each country. It thus might be misleading to generalize the effect of trade on openness in one economy to other economies, even when their characteristics are rather similar.

Harrison (1996) provides ways to address the measurement error and cross-sectional analysis controversy. He uses seven different measures to proxy the degree of openness of each country. The analysis covers the period 1960–1988 for 51 countries. A long-run average cross-sectional analysis and a cross-country time series panel analysis are both conducted. From the former method we find that (i) only 1 of the 7 openness indices enters the growth regression with a positive and statistically significant coefficient, (ii) 3 of the 7 indices affect growth positively when average five-year data are analyzed, and (iii) 6 of the 7 indices become statistically significant when annual data are considered. Hence, the study accentuates the importance of a time-series approach in analyzing the trade and growth relationship.

Jin (2000) studies the short-run dynamics of trade openness and economic growth in six East Asian economies by analyzing time-series data for each country. He employs a five-variable VAR model incorporating GDP, money supply, government spending, foreign price, and openness. Impulse response functions (IRF) and variance decompositions (VDC) are computed to look at the effects of trade on growth. From the IRFs, he finds that the short-run output impacts of trade are positive but small and insignificant for five countries. From the VDCs, the forecast error variance of GDP explained by the trade openness innovation is also small and insignificant for the five countries. The effects of the shocks on government spending and foreign price are more substantial.

Hatemi and Irandoust (2001) study the direction of causality between export and productivity in five OECD countries. First, the Johansen method suggests the existence of one cointegrating vector between export and productivity. Then, the Granger causality test augmented with the error-correction term is carried out for each country. Although the results are rather disparate, causality generally runs from export to productivity. VDCs between export and total factor productivity (TFP) are also computed. The export innovations explain around 3% of the forecast error variance of TFP in France, 48% in Germany, 42% in Italy, 80% in Sweden, and 86% in the UK.

Van Den Berg (1996) addresses the causality controversy in six Latin American countries by comparing results from single equation and simultaneous equation models. He argues the following: first, that imports and exports both have positive and distinct effects on economic growth; second, that there is simultaneity between trade and growth; and finally, that the impacts of openness on growth are higher and more significant in the simultaneous equation model than in the single equation model.[1]

2.2.2 Con's

Theoretical skepticism about the effect of trade openness on income is based essentially on two premises, as put forward by Prebisch (1950) and

---

[1] However, Afxentiou and Serletis (2000) do not find any causal relationship between exports or imports and growth.

Singer (1950). First, incessant decreases in the international prices of raw materials and primary commodities would lead, without industrialization in developing countries, to more profound differences between developed and developing countries. Second, developing economies require short- or medium-term protection of their infant industries in order to industrialize.

Krugman (1994) and Rodrik (1995), amongst others, argue that outward policy has little to no effect on growth.

Rodriguez and Rodrik (1999) argue that effect of trade on growth cannot be unambiguously signed. The impact is positive if the resource allocation effects of trade policy promote sectors that generate more long-run growth, and negative otherwise.

Skepticism about the effect of trade on economic growth is stronger for the case of African economies. The structure of trade under which exports are concentrated on a few primary products and imports are constituted mostly by manufactured goods, renders those economies overly dependent and vulnerable. Because of the low price elasticity of African exports and the contained demand for primary products in the international market, African economies face continuously decreasing terms of trade.

Among the few empirical studies on the trade and growth relationship in Africa, Rodrik (1998) focuses on the role of trade and trade policy in achieving sustained long-term growth in sub-Saharan Africa. His first conclusion is that trade policy in sub-Saharan Africa works in much the same way it does elsewhere. Stringent trade restrictions have been important obstacles to exports in the past, and an easing of restrictions can be expected to significantly improve the trade performance in the region. Going against the thoughts mentioned above, however, his paper argues that there are no grounds to presume that Africa's divergent conditions, poor infrastructure, geography, or dependence on limited numbers of primary goods for export and manufactured goods for import make the region an exceptional case where exports remain unresponsive to prices or instruments of trade policy. As a second and major conclusion in his paper, Rodrik (1998) asserts that trade policy has only small and indirect effects on economic growth. An increase in the share of income exported was proven to not, in itself, contribute to growth in per-capita income. Besides, none of the trade policy indexes, the Sachs-Warner openness index, import taxes and black market premium entered the growth regression significantly. Rodrik (1998) showed that the role of trade policy in economic growth is largely auxiliary and of an enabling nature: sharply increased export taxation and import restrictions can suffocate economic activities in their beginnings, while an open trade policy will not, on its own, set an economy on a sustained path of growth.

2.3 Data

We investigate the trade and growth relationship in sub-Saharan African countries and in selected developing countries in Asia and Latin America. All sub-Saharan African countries with available data are included. Two criteria have been used to select the Latin American and Asian countries included in the study: (i) the per capita incomes of the selected countries were within the range of the minimum and maximum per capita incomes of the sub-Saharan African economies at the beginning of the study period (1960), and (ii) the selected countries achieved somewhat higher growth performance compared to the sub-Saharan African economies. As a result, we use the data of following countries.

Sub-Saharan African countries: Benin; Botswana; Burkina Faso; Burundi; Cameroon; Chad; Comoros; Democratic Republic of the Congo; Republic of the Congo; Côte d'Ivoire; Gabon; Gambia; Ghana; Guinea Bissau; Kenya; Lesotho; Madagascar; Malawi; Mali; Mauritius; Mozambique; Nigeria; Rwanda; Senegal; Sierra Leone; South Africa; Swaziland; Togo; Zambia; Zimbabwe.

Asian countries: Hong Kong; Korea; Philippines; Malaysia; Thailand; Indonesia.

Latin American countries: Brazil; Mexico; Bolivia; Colombia; Costa Rica; Paraguay; Uruguay; Dominican Republic; Ecuador; El Salvador; Venezuela.

The empirical results will be compared to assess the specific characteristics of the African economies.

Trade is proxied with the share of imports and exports to GDP. Though the trade share continues to be severely criticized as a measure of the openness of an economy, we take this proxy for two reasons. First, alternative measures are not available on a long-term basis. Without such alternatives, an appropriate time-series analysis cannot be conducted. Second, the trade share appears to have the highest correlation coefficients with other proxies, among the indexes of trade openness.[2]

Hence, the variables introduced in the model are real gross domestic product (GDP) in 1995 prices and trade share, both in logarithmic form.

We use annual data from 1960 to 2001, but the sample period is shortened for countries with no data available for the entire sample. We attempt to extensively use information embodied in the data. Unlike most studies that apply the cross-section approach to focus on this topic, we use the time series of each country and apply a variance decomposition analysis.

[2] As in Harisson (1996), the trade share generally shows the largest correlation coefficients with a high significance level. Stryker and Pandolfi (1998) also choose the trade share for their analysis of sub-Saharan African economies.

2.4 Empirical Techniques

The variance decomposition (VDC) technique computes the percentage of the forecast variance of one variable accounted for by one other variable introduced in the model.[3]

Let us explain the procedure of variance decomposition based on the bivariate VAR model. If the variables constituting the vector $y_t = [Y_{1,t}\ Y_{2,t}]'$ are stationary, we can transform the VAR (vector autoregression) in vector moving average representation using the following procedure. We start with

$$y_t = \Phi_0 + \Phi_1 y_{t-1} + u_t, \tag{2.1}$$

where u_t is the vector of error terms with zero mean and finite variance. Then, we use a lag operator L to get

$$(I - \Phi_1 L)y_t = \Phi_0 + u_t. \tag{2.2}$$

This gives us

$$\begin{aligned} y_t &= (I - \Phi_1 L)^{-1}\Phi_0 + (I - \Phi_1 L)^{-1} u_t \\ &= (I - \Phi_1 L)^{-1}\Phi_0 + \sum_{i=0}^{\infty} \Phi_1^i u_{t-i} \\ &= \Psi_0 + \sum_{i=0}^{\infty} \Psi_i u_{t-i}, \end{aligned} \tag{2.3}$$

where $\Psi_0 = (I - \Phi_1 L)^{-1}\Phi_0$ and $\Psi_i = \Phi_1^i$.

Updating (2.3) n periods, we obtain

$$y_{t+n} = \Psi_0 + \sum_{i=0}^{\infty} \Psi_i u_{t+n-i}. \tag{2.4}$$

If we take conditional expectation of (2.4), the n-step-ahead forecast of y_{t+n} is

$$E(y_{t+n} \mid I_t) = \Psi_0 + \sum_{i=n}^{\infty} \Psi_i u_{t+n-i}, \tag{2.5}$$

where $E(\bullet \mid I_t)$ is the conditional expectations operator given the information available at time t, and $I_t = (y_t, u_t, y_{t-1}, u_{t-1}, \cdots)$ is the information set available at time t. Thus, the n-period forecast error $y_{t+n} - E(y_{t+n} \mid I_t)$ is

[3] Enders (2004) is a good reference for applied time series analysis.

$$y_{t+n} - E(y_{t+n} \mid I_t) = \sum_{i=0}^{n-1} \Psi_i u_{t+n-i}. \tag{2.6}$$

It follows from (2.6) that the n-step-ahead forecast errors of $Y_{1,t}$ and $Y_{2,t}$ are respectively given as

$$\begin{aligned} Y_{1,t+n} - E(Y_{1,t+n} \mid I_t) = u_{1,t+n} &+ \psi_{11}(1)u_{1,t+n-1} + \cdots + \psi_{11}(n-1)u_{1,t+1} \\ &+ \psi_{12}(1)u_{2,t+n-1} + \cdots + \psi_{12}(n-1)u_{2,t+1}, \end{aligned} \tag{2.7}$$

and

$$\begin{aligned} Y_{2,t+n} - E(Y_{2,t+n} \mid I_t) = u_{2,t+n} &+ \psi_{21}(1)u_{1,t+n-1} + \cdots + \psi_{21}(n-1)u_{1,t+1} \\ &+ \psi_{22}(1)u_{2,t+n-1} + \cdots + \psi_{22}(n-1)u_{2,t+1}. \end{aligned} \tag{2.8}$$

If we take conditional variance of (2.7) and (2.8), the n-step-ahead forecast error variances of $Y_{1,t}$ and $Y_{2,t}$ are respectively given as

$$\begin{aligned} V(Y_{1,t+n} \mid I_t) = \sigma_1^2&[1 + \psi_{11}(1)^2 + \ldots + \psi_{11}(n-1)^2] \\ &+ \sigma_2^2[\psi_{12}(1)^2 + \ldots + \psi_{12}(n-1)^2], \end{aligned} \tag{2.9}$$

and

$$\begin{aligned} V(Y_{2,t+n} \mid I_t) = \sigma_1^2&[\psi_{21}(1)^2 + \ldots + \psi_{21}(n-1)^2] \\ &+ \sigma_2^2[1 + \psi_{22}(1)^2 + \ldots + \psi_{22}(n-1)^2], \end{aligned} \tag{2.10}$$

where $V(Y_{j,t+n} \mid I_t) = E[\{Y_{j,t+n} - E(Y_{j,t+n} \mid I_t)\}^2 \mid I_t]$ $(j = 1,2)$ is a conditional variance given the information available at time t and

$$\Psi_k = \begin{bmatrix} \psi_{11}(k) & \psi_{12}(k) \\ \psi_{21}(k) & \psi_{22}(k) \end{bmatrix}.$$

Now it is possible to decompose the n-step-ahead forecast error variance into the proportion due to each shock. Thus, the relative variance contribution (RVC) is defined as follows:

$$RVC(Y_j \to Y_i : n) = \frac{\sum_{k=0}^{n-1} \psi_{ij}(k)^2 \sigma_j^2}{V_t(Y_{i,t+n})} \quad i, j = 1,2, \tag{2.11}$$

which sums up to 100%. The forecast error variance decomposition tells us the proportion of the movements in a sequence due to its own shocks versus shocks to the other variable.

2.5 Empirical Results

As a preliminary analysis, we check the order of integration of each variable. We use the augmented Dickey-Fuller (ADF) test for this purpose (Dickey and Fuller, 1979). As a result, both of GDP and trade share are found to have a unit root for most cases. We then proceed to the Engle-Granger cointegration test (Engle and Granger, 1987). As we find no cointegration for almost all countries, we generalize that the GDP and trade share are not cointegrated.

Hence, we estimate the bivariate VAR for the growth rate of GDP and trade share, and compute the share of the forecast variance of aggregate economic growth accounted for by the trade share. Table 2.1 gives the results of this variance decomposition analysis. As clearly seen from the table, the share of forecast variance of GDP growth accounted for by trade after twenty periods exceeds 10% in 21 out of the 30 sub-Saharan African countries examined. For Asia, the share exceeds 10% in none of the 6 countries. For Latin America, the share exceeds 10% in 3 out of the 11 countries.

In brief, it is confirmed that (i) trade openness influence markedly growth, (ii) economic growth is particularly sensitive to trade in sub-Saharan African economies compared to the examined Asian and Latin American economies. Therefore, it is necessary to find out measures that will lead to the broadening of the countries' participation in international trade. Sharpening international competitiveness is at the core of such measures.

Table 2.1. Variance decomposition

	Trade share	GDP
Africa		
Benin	11.809	88.191
Botswana	37.711	62.289
Burkina Faso	5.965	94.035
Burundi	3.033	96.967
Cameroon	12.459	87.541
Chad	22.888	77.112
Comoros	9.571	90.429
Congo Dem. Rep.	4.404	95.596
Congo Rep.	14.585	85.415
Côte d'Ivoire	12.196	87.804
Gabon	4.466	95.534

Table 2.1. (cont.)

	Trade share	GDP
Gambia	16.793	83.207
Ghana	19.952	80.048
Guinea Bissau	12.017	87.983
Kenya	0.350	99.650
Lesotho	21.992	78.008
Madagascar	12.670	87.330
Malawi	25.895	74.105
Mali	32.231	67.769
Mauritius	28.431	71.569
Mozambique	14.919	85.081
Nigeria	0.702	99.298
Rwanda	48.764	51.236
Senegal	2.979	97.021
Sierra Leone	39.375	60.625
South Africa	18.336	81.664
Swaziland	9.917	90.083
Togo	13.329	86.671
Zambia	21.000	79.000
Zimbabwe	22.248	77.752
Asia		
Hong Kong	8.077	91.923
Korea	3.310	96.690
Philippines	0.136	99.864
Malaysia	3.201	96.799
Thailand	1.782	98.218
Indonesia	1.992	98.008
Latin America		
Brazil	2.466	97.534
Mexico	22.322	77.678
Bolivia	4.063	95.937
Colombia	9.685	90.315
Costa Rica	16.862	83.138
Paraguay	19.798	80.202
Uruguay	2.087	97.913
Dominican Rep.	9.965	90.035
Ecuador	2.457	97.543
El Salvador	5.732	94.268
Venezuela	3.265	96.735

Note: The values in the table show the decomposition of the forecast variance of GDP accounted for by the GDP and the Trade Share in the 20th period.

2.6 Conclusion

In this chapter we have empirically analyzed the relationship between the trade share and economic growth using variance decomposition. Our major conclusions can be summarized as follows:

(1) Trade accounts for a large share of the forecast variance of GDP growth in African countries. The share after 20 periods exceeds 10% for two-thirds of the 30 African countries and exceeds 20% for more than one-third of those countries.

(2) Interestingly, the computed VDCs reveal that the influence of trade on GDP is generally larger in sub-Saharan African economies than in Latin American and Asian economies. The share of forecast variance of GDP accounted for by trade exceeds 10% in only 3 out of the 11 Latin American countries studied and fails to reach the 10% level in any of the 6 Asian economies studied.

Hence, trade policy offers large room and can serve as a powerful tool for policymakers working to foster economic growth in sub-Saharan African economies.

Following this analysis of the trade and growth relationship, the next chapter turns to the second channel of participation in globalization, namely, Foreign Direct Investment, and analyzes its effect on economic growth.

References

Afxentiou, P.C. and Serletis, A. (2000) Output growth and the variability of export and import growth: international evidence from Granger causality tests, *Developing Economies*, **38**, 141-65.

Coe, D.T., Helpman, E. and Hoffmaister, A.W. (1997) North-South R&D spillovers, *Economic Journal*, **107**, 134-149.

Dickey, D. and Fuller, W.A. (1979), Distribution of the estimates for autoregressive time series with a unit root, *Journal of the American Statistical Association*, **74**, 427-31.

Edwards, S. (1998) Openness, productivity and growth: what do we really know? *Economic Journal*, **108**, 383-398.

Enders, W. (2004) *Applied Econometric Time Series*, 2nd edn. John Wiley & Sons Inc, New York.

Engle, R.F. and Granger, C.W.J. (1987), Cointegration and error correction: representation, estimation and testing, *Econometrica*, **55**, 251-276.

Esfahani, H.S. (1991) Exports, imports, and economic growth in semi-industrialized countries, *Journal of Development Economics*, **35**, 93-116.

Feder, G. (1982) On exports and economic growth, *Journal of Development Economics*, **12**, 59-73.

Frankel, J.A. and Romer, D. (1996) Trade and growth: an empirical investigation, NBER Working Paper 5476, National Bureau of Economic Research, Inc.

Grossman, G.M. and Helpman, E. (1991) *Innovation and Growth in the Global Economy*, MIT Press: Cambridge, MA.

Harrison, A. (1996) Openness and growth: a time series, cross-country analysis for developing countries, *Journal of Development Economics*, **48**, 419-47.

Hatemi, A.J. and Irandoust, M. (2001) Productivity performance and export performance: a time series perspective, *Eastern Economic Journal*, **27**, 149-164.

Jin, J.C. (2000) Openness and growth: an interpretation of empirical evidence from East Asian countries, *Journal of International Trade and Economic Development*, **9**, 5-17.

Krugman, P. (1994) Competitiveness: a dangerous obsession, *Foreign Affairs*, **73**, 28-44

Kruger, A. (1978) *Foreign Trade Regimes and Economic Development: Liberalization Attempts and Consequences*, Ballinger Publish Co. for NBER: Cambridge, MA.

Lucas, R.E.Jr. (1988) On the mechanics of economic development, *Journal of Monetary Economics*, **22**, 3-42.

Prebisch, R. (1950) *The Economic Development of Latin America and its Principal. Problems*, United Nations: New York.

Rodriguez, F. and Rodrik, D. (1999) Trade policy and economic growth: a skeptic's guide to cross-national evidence, NBER Working Papers 7081, National Bureau of Economic Research, Inc.

Rodrik, D. (1995) Trade and industrial policy reform in developing countries: a review of theory and evidence, chap. 45 in *Handbook of Development Economics*, Volume 3B, Holland, Elsevier Science.

Rodrik, D. (1998) Trade policy and economic performance in Sub-Saharan Africa, NBER Working Papers 6562, National Bureau of Economic Research, Inc.

Romer, P.M. (1986) Increasing returns and long-run growth, *Journal of Political Economy*, **94**, 1002-1037.

Singer, H.W. (1950) U.S. foreign investment in underdeveloped areas: the distribution of gains between investing and borrowing countries, *American Economic Review, Papers and Proceedings*, **40**, 473-485.

Solow, R.M. (1956) A contribution to the theory of economic growth, *Quarterly Journal of Economics*, **70**, 65-94.

Stryker, D.J. and Pandolfi, S. (1998) Effects of policy reform on investment, trade and growth in Sub-Saharan Africa, United States Agency for International Development (USAID).

Van Den Berg, H. (1996) Does simultaneity distort tests of the trade-growth relationship? *Applied Economics Letters*, **3**, 225-231.

Wacziarg, R. (2001) Measuring the dynamic gains from trade, *World Bank Economic Review*, **15**, 393-429.

3 FDI and Economic Growth

3.1 Introduction

Foreign direct investment (FDI) becomes crucial for many developing countries. FDI has some potentially desirable features that affect the growth with significant implications for poverty reduction. Thus, this is an important issue particularly in the case of sub-Saharan African countries with a small share of FDI inflows relatively to other developing countries. This chapter empirically analyzes the relationship between foreign direct investment (FDI) and economic growth (Fig. 3.1).

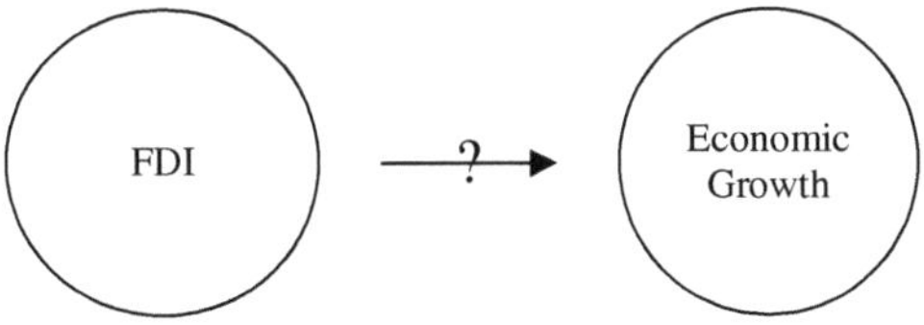

Fig. 3.1. FDI and economic growth

3.2 Literature Review

The literature on FDI and growth relationship can be classified into two groups: (i) studies that emphasizing favorable contributions of FDI on growth, what we qualify as "Pro's," and (ii) studies that emphasize either weak or even harmful effects of FDI on growth, what we call "Con's."

3.2.1 Pro's

According to the neoclassical growth theory, long-run economic growth stems from technological progress and labor force growth, factors assumed to be exogenous. Under this assumption, FDI can only be expected to have a short-run effect on output growth. However, the recent development of endogenous growth theory has encouraged researchers to analyze the channels through which FDI promotes economic growth in the long-run (Grossman and Helpman, 1991).

The impact of FDI on economic growth is postulated to run through two channels. First, FDI is expected to stimulate economic growth by encouraging the incorporation of new inputs and foreign technologies in the production function of the host country through capital accumulation. Second, FDI is expected to augment the level of knowledge in the host country through labor training, skill acquisition, and the introduction of alternative management practices and organizational arrangements.

On this basis, FDI can be seen as a vehicle for industrial development and technological progress. By increasing productivity and technological progress in a host country, foreign investors might therefore have positive impacts on economic growth. In developing countries in particular, a combination of advanced management skills and newer technologies is likely to increase the efficiency of FDI. Indeed, FDI may be the main channel through which advanced technology is transferred to developing countries (Borensztein et al., 1998, p. 133).

The works by Balasubramanyam et al. (1996) and Borensztein et al. (1998) are prominent among the empirical studies on the relationship between FDI and economic growth.

Balasubramanyam et al. (1996) employ a new growth theory framework to examine the role of FDI in the growth of developing countries with different trade policy regimes. Using annual average data on a cross-section of 46 developing countries from 1970 to 1985, they demonstrate empirically that FDI has a positive and significant effect on economic growth. They also show that FDI enhances economic growth more robustly in countries that promote exports (e.g. Singapore, Malaysia, South Korea, and Chile) than in countries that adopt import substitution policies (e.g. Bangladesh, Peru, Philippines, and Mexico).

Borensztein et al. (1998) empirically test the effect of foreign direct investment (FDI) on economic growth in a cross-country regression framework using data on 69 developing countries between 1970 and 1989. Their results suggest that FDI is an important vehicle for the transfer of technology and that it contributes relatively more to growth than domestic investment. They also find that the effect of FDI on economic growth depends on the level of human capital available in the host economy.

Many of the existing studies on this subject make that prior presumption that FDI responds to or causes economic growth. Few, however, consider the feedback relationship between FDI and economic growth. To strike a better balance, there have been several attempts to focus more closely on the causal relationship between FDI and growth using different samples and estimation techniques. Noteworthy among these are the studies by Zhang (2001), Ericsson and Irandoust (2001), and Chowdhury and Mavrots (2003).

Zhang (2001) empirically analyzes the relationship between FDI and economic growth in developing countries using data on 11 economies in East Asia and Latin America. He finds that FDI can be expected to boost economic growth in the host country, but the extent of this growth-enhancing effect appears to depend on country-specific characteristics. He also finds that FDI is more likely to promote economic growth when host countries adopt liberalized trade regimes, improve education (and thereby human capital conditions), encourage export-oriented FDI, and maintain macro-economic stability.

Ericsson and Irandoust (2001) empirically examine the causal relationship between FDI and economic growth in Denmark, Finland, Norway, and Sweden using annual data between 1970 and 1997. Their analysis is based on the LA-VAR (lag-augmented vector autoregression) procedure developed by Toda and Yamamoto (1995). They find that the causal link is bi-directional for Sweden, uni-directional from FDI to economic growth for Norway, and unsupportable for Finland and Denmark.

Chowdhury and Mavrots (2003) empirically analyze the causal relationship between FDI and economic growth in three developing countries, i.e. Chile, Malaysia, and Thailand. They analyze the issue by applying the LA-VAR procedure using annual data between 1969 and 2000. Their empirical results provide strong evidence of a bi-directional causality between GDP and FDI for Malaysia and Thailand, and of a unidirectional causality from GDP to FDI for Chile.

3.2.2 Con's

The most intense debate on the possible adverse effects of FDI on economic growth has centered on the economic circumstances of the recipient economy. Human capital and the financial markets in the host country may influence the FDI effects.

Borensztein et al. (1998) stress the importance of human capital in the host country. They suggest that the FDI effects on economic growth depend on the level of human capital available. Their empirical results indicate that the higher productivity of FDI holds only when the host country has a minimum threshold stock of human capital. If they are correct, FDI can only be expected to contribute to economic growth when the host economy has a sufficient capability to absorb advanced technologies.

Alfaro et al. (2004) point out that local financial markets must be sufficiently developed if FDI is to enhance economic growth. They empirically analyze the link among FDI, financial markets, and economic growth using cross-country data between 1975 and 1995. Their empirical results show that FDI alone plays an ambiguous role in contributing to economic growth overall. In countries with well-developed financial markets, on the other hand, they find that the gains from FDI are significant. They also provide evidence of a causal link between FDI and growth, whereby FDI promotes growth through financial markets.

Durham (2004) examines the effects of FDI on economic growth using data on 80 countries from 1979 through 1998. His empirical results suggest that the FDI effects on economic growth are contingent on the absorptive capacity of the host country, particularly with respect to financial and institutional development.

The crowding-out effect is another of the possible adverse effects of FDI on a domestic economy. If domestic firms lack sufficient competitiveness compared to foreign firms, they can be pushed out of the market and forced to cease their activities. The crowding-out effect results essentially from the competition between FDI and domestic firms in the local goods and factor markets (labor, financial market). If the inflow of FDI is more productive and produces higher value added than the domestic firms and forces the domestic firms to shift to activities which produce value added at least as large as that of their foreign competitors, then the crowding-out effect might benefit the economy overall. This phenomenon is qualified as "constructive destruction." Borensztein et al. (1998) report evidence in support of a crowding-in effect, namely, that FDI is complementary to domestic investment.[1]

3.3 Data

We investigate the FDI and growth relationship in sub-Saharan African countries and in selected developing countries in Asia and Latin America. All sub-Saharan African countries with available data are included. Two criteria have been used to select the Latin American and Asian countries included in the study: (i) the per capita incomes of the selected countries were within the range of the minimum and maximum per capita incomes of the sub-Saharan African economies at the beginning of the study period (1960), and (ii) the selected countries achieved somewhat higher growth performance compared to the sub-Saharan African economies. As a result, we use the data of following countries.

Sub-Saharan African countries: Benin; Botswana; Burkina Faso; Burundi; Cameroon; Chad; Comoros; Democratic Republic of the Congo; Republic of the Congo; Côte d'Ivoire; Gabon; Gambia; Ghana; Guinea Bissau; Kenya;

[1] De Gregorio (1992) reports that FDI is about three times more efficient than domestic investment using a panel data of 12 Latin American countries.

Lesotho; Madagascar; Malawi; Mali; Mauritius; Mozambique; Nigeria; Rwanda; Senegal; Sierra Leone; South Africa; Swaziland; Togo; Zambia; Zimbabwe.

Asian countries: Hong Kong; Korea; Philippines; Malaysia; Thailand; Indonesia.

Latin American countries: Brazil; Mexico; Bolivia; Colombia; Costa Rica; Paraguay; Uruguay; Dominican Republic; Ecuador; El Salvador; Venezuela.

The empirical results will be compared to assess the specific characteristics of the African economies. Annual data from 1980 to 2001 are employed.

We measure the foreign investments as the real inward stock of FDI rather than as the FDI inflows because of two reasons: (i) all of the existing FDI in the host-country (not solely the FDI recently invested) is included in the aggregate capital for the production of GDP; (ii) all of the existing FDI in the host-country (not solely the FDI recently invested) embodies higher know-how and technology.

Hence, real GDP (USD 1995 prices) and inward stock of FDI are included in the model. Data on real GDP are taken from the World Development Indicators of the World Bank (2003); the real inward stock of FDI is computed from the nominal inward stock of FDI obtained from the Global Development Finance (2003), and deflated with the World Consumer Price Index drawn from the International Financial Statistics of the International Monetary Fund (June 2004).

3.4 Empirical Analysis

3.4.1 Variance Decomposition

Following the discussion of Chap. 2, we analyze the relationship between FDI and economic growth using the variance decomposition (VDC) techniques.[2]

As a preliminary analysis, we carry out the unit root test to check the order of integration of each variable. We adopt the commonly employed augmented Dickey-Fuller (ADF) test for this purpose (Dickey and Fuller, 1979). As a result, both of FDI and economic growth rates are found to be stationary for most cases.

Then, after constructing a bivariate vector autoregression (VAR) model for each country, we apply the VDC technique on the growth rate of GDP and the growth rate of the inward stock of FDI. The forecast error variance

[2] Enders (2004) is a good reference for applied time series analysis.

decomposition tells us the proportion of the movements in a sequence due to its own shocks versus shocks to the other variable.

The decomposition of the forecast variance of GDP growth displayed in Table 3.1 gives us insight into the share accounted for by FDI. We can deduce the following findings from these results.

1. FDI accounts for a large share of the forecast variance of GDP in most of the countries investigated.
2. FDI accounts for more than 10% of the forecast variance of GDP in 16 out of the 30 sub-Saharan African countries examined, and for more than 15% in 9 of the countries.
3. In contrast to our earlier findings on the trade-growth relationship in Chap. 2, our findings on the pattern of the FDI-growth relationship in the sub-Saharan Africa economies do not clearly differ from those in Asian and Latin American economies. This suggests that foreign investments might affect growth in the SSA economies via patterns somewhat similar to those of the FDI effects in other economies, i.e. mainly in terms of time-lengths and magnitudes.

Table 3.1. Variance decomposition

	FDI	GDP
Africa		
Benin	14.762	85.238
Botswana	11.576	88.424
Burkina Faso	11.126	88.874
Burundi	8.923	91.077
Cameroon	16.263	83.737
Chad	4.954	95.046
Comoros	0.569	99.431
Congo Dem. Rep	10.799	89.201
Congo Rep.	0.887	99.113
Côte d'Ivoire	16.570	83.430
Gabon	2.833	97.167
Gambia	18.411	81.589
Ghana	2.466	97.534
Guinea Bissau	2.133	97.867
Kenya	19.657	80.343
Lesotho	1.205	98.795
Madagascar	14.191	85.809
Malawi	1.387	98.613
Mali	1.860	98.140
Mauritius	67.614	32.386
Mozambique	16.009	83.991

Table 3.1. (cont.)

	FDI	GDP
Nigeria	0.946	99.054
Rwanda	28.362	71.638
Senegal	22.757	77.243
Sierra Leone	13.620	86.380
South Africa	5.150	94.850
Swaziland	12.979	87.021
Togo	11.373	88.627
Zambia	42.085	57.915
Zimbabwe	0.769	99.231
Asia		
Hong Kong	1.689	98.311
Korea	4.092	95.908
Philippines	0.583	99.417
Malaysia	5.410	94.590
Thailand	46.304	53.696
Indonesia	19.454	80.546
Latin America		
Brazil	4.844	95.156
Mexico	13.759	86.241
Bolivia	33.026	66.974
Colombia	78.346	21.654
Costa Rica	7.937	92.063
Paraguay	19.082	80.918
Uruguay	9.204	90.796
Dominican Rep.	53.895	46.105
Ecuador	6.469	93.531
El Salvador	1.415	98.585
Venezuela	4.908	95.092

Note: The values in the table represent the decomposition of the forecast variance of GDP accounted for by GDP and FDI in the 10th period.

4. FDI has been seen as an engine of the rapid growth in some of the Asian and Latin American economies presently selected, whereas the inward stock of FDI in Africa is relatively low. Given that economic growth is as sensitive to FDI in Africa as it is in Asia and Latin America, an enhanced level of FDI might contribute vigorously to economic growth in the sub-Saharan African economies examined.

3.4.2 Causality Tests

We examine the direction of causality between FDI and income in the economies of sub-Saharan Africa for two purposes. Our first purpose is to strengthen our statement that FDI enhances growth. Our second purpose relates to the implications of earlier findings. Some studies assert that FDI firms tend to operate more actively in medium-income countries than in less developed economies, because of the advantages of better developed infrastructure and other factors. Inherent in this is the assumption that up to a certain level, causality runs from development or GDP to FDI inflow.

To benefit from the information embodied in the panel structure of the data, we apply the panel-data-based Granger causality test suggested by Hurlin and Venet (2001). Hurlin and Venet (2001) extended the Granger causality test methodology developed for time series models to panel data. Different maximum lag lengths are used (from lag one to five) to verify the accuracy of the inference. Table 3.2 displays the results. Three findings stand out from the results given.

1. All models from the five different lag lengths confirm that FDI Granger causes economic growth in the sub-Saharan African economies.
2. Only two of the five models depicts a causal relationship from economic growth to FDI in those African countries.
3. The panel-data-based causality test confirms the finding from the VDC analysis, namely, that FDI policy can serve as a strong tool for fostering economic growth in Africa.

Table 3.2. Panel causality test, GDP – FDI in Africa

Lag	From FDI to GDP	From GDP to FDI
1	17.208***	5.804**
2	10.381***	21.094***
3	8.412***	2.11
4	5.368***	2.647
5	7 658***	1.489

Note: ***(**) indicate the significance level at 1%(5%)

3.5 Conclusion

In this chapter, we empirically analyze the relationship between FDI and economic growth. Our work confirms the following in the sub-Saharan African economies examined: (i) foreign investments markedly influence growth and (ii) the direction of causality runs uni-directionally from foreign investments to economic growth. Henceforth it will be necessary to identify measures that can be expected to increase the inward stock of foreign investments. Sharpening international competitiveness will be at the core of such measures. The ensuing chapters focus on the effectiveness of policy measures in bringing about stronger competitiveness, both in international trade and in foreign direct investment.

References

Alfaro, L., Chanda, A., Kalemli-Ozcan, S. and Sayek, S. (2004) FDI and economic growth: the role of local financial markets, *Journal of International Economics*, **64**, 89-112.

Balasubramanyam, V.N., Salisu, M. and Sapsford, D. (1996) Foreign direct investment and growth in EP and IS countries, *Economic Journal*, **106**, 92-105.

Borensztein, E., Gregorio, J.De and Lee, J-W. (1998) How does foreign direct investment affect economic growth? *Journal of International Economics*, **45**, 115-135.

Chowdhury, A. and Mavrots, G. (2003) FDI and growth: what causes what ?, Paper presented at the WIDER Conference, Helsinki, Finland.

De Gregorio, J. (1992) Economic growth in Latin America, *Journal of Development Economics*, **39**, 58-84.

Dickey, D. and Fuller, W.A. (1979) Distribution of the estimates for autoregressive time series with a unit root, *Journal of the American Statistical Association*, **74**, 427-31.

Durham, J.B. (2004) Absorptive capacity and the effects of foreign direct investment and equity foreign portfolio investment on economic growth, *European Economic Review*, **48**, 285-306.

Enders, W. (2004) *Applied Econometric Time Series*, 2nd edn. John Wiley & Sons Inc, New York.

Ericsson, J., and Irandoust, M. (2001) On the causality between foreign direct investment and output: a comparative study, *International Trade Journal*, **15**, 1-26.

Grossman, G.M. and Helpman, E. (1991) *Innovation and Growth in the Global Economy*, MIT Press, Cambridge, MA.

Hurlin, C. and Venet, B. (2001) Granger causality tests in Panel data models with fixed coefficients, Working Paper, EURISCO, Universit'e Paris IX Dauphine.

Toda, H. and Yamamoto, T. (1995) Statistical inference in vector autoregressions with possibly integrated processes, *Journal of Econometrics*, **66,** 225-250.

Zhang, K.H., (2001) Does FDI promote economic growth? evidence from East Asia and Latin America, *Contemporary Economic Policy*, **19**, 175-185.

4 Trade Competitiveness: Exchange Rate and Inflation

4.1 Introduction

In keeping with the Ricardian theory and the Heckscher–Ohlin theorem, economists originally associated a country's international participation with its pattern of comparative advantage. The concept of comparative advantage can be explained in simple terms. A country specializes in the production of goods or services that it can provide at lower relative prices. Lower relative prices result from the intensive use of relatively abundant factor endowments or the development of better technologies for the production of goods or services in the sector in which the country holds a comparative advantage. By leading each participant to seek out and exploit its comparative advantage, trade improves the allocation of resources among participants and ultimately improves the welfare of each. The theory of comparative advantage was originally presented in a static setting; in other words, the analysis was conducted in terms of the "existing" factor endowments.

Later on, economists extended the analysis to a dynamic setting and established the concept of "dynamic comparative advantage." The "dynamic" dimension of this concept is the tendency of the factor endowments of a country to change through participation in international trade. As one example, the growth-enhancing effects of international trade can positively influence the gross capital formation of a country and thereby alter the capital-labor ratio. International trade can also heighten the ratio between skilled and non-skilled labor. These types of transformation will differ from one country to another, which in turn will change the patterns of comparative advantages among the countries.

Subsequently, recent studies on international trade have incorporated the concepts of competitive advantage and competitiveness into the framework of static and dynamic comparative advantage. As Porter (1990) pointed out, the competitiveness of countries has become a major concern not only among researchers, but more importantly, among policymakers. Researchers and policymakers now understand that higher competitiveness in international trade lies at the core of intensifying participation in international trade. Put more simply, a more competitive country can trade on a larger scale.

In this chapter we classify the published studies on international trade into two groups based on their approaches to trade competitiveness. The first group is comprised of what we describe as "Pro's," namely, studies that consider and emphasize the importance of trade competitiveness and the use of policy tools to strengthen it. The second group is made up of what we describe as the "Con's," namely, analyses that consider competitiveness at the sectoral level while dismissing it as less "less meaningful" at the national level. By the "Con's" line of reasoning, any enhancement in participation in international trade should be based solely on comparative advantage.

4.2 Literature Review

4.2.1 Pro's

Various groups of researchers and policymakers, including those affiliated with international organizations involved in development assistance, have touted the importance of international competitiveness. The strengthening of international competitiveness is advocated as a way to foster economic growth through openness. Trade competitiveness at the national level has been variously defined in the literature (Aiginger, 1998, Table 1):

- The ability to sell.
- The ability to sell products on international markets, while incomes in the domestic markets increase in a sustainable way (Competitiveness Policy Council, 1994).
- The ability to create the preconditions for high wages.
- The ability to develop specialty products and technical solutions which generate income growth under full employment, in spite of the emerging competition of the newly industrialized countries.
- A nation state's ability to produce, distribute, and service goods in the international economy, and to do so in a way that earns a rising standard of living (Scott and Lodge, 1985, p.15).
- The ability of a country to realize central economic policy goals, especially growth in income and employment, without running into balance-of-payment difficulties (Fagerberg, 1988, p.355).

- The only meaningful concept of competitiveness at the national level is national productivity (Porter, 1990, p.6ff.).
- To produce goods and services which meet the test of foreign competition while simultaneously maintaining and expanding domestic real income (OECD/TEP, 1992, p.237).
- Competitiveness as the ability to combine growth with balanced trade.
- World competitiveness is the ability of a country or a company to proportionally generate more wealth than its competitors in the world markets.
- The ability to increase or to maintain the living standard relative to comparable economies (e.g. developed industrialized countries) without long-run deterioration of external balance.
- Competitive policy...supports the ability of companies, industries, regions and nations or supra-national regions to generate relatively high factor income and factor employment levels on a sustainable basis while remaining exposed to international competition (OECD, 1995a, p.8).
- Competitiveness policy seeks to enhance the competitiveness of nations by supporting the ability of companies, industries, regions, nations, or supra-national regions to generate relatively high factor income and factor employment levels while remaining opposed to international competition (OECD, 1995b, p.3).
- Historians have tended to equate competitiveness ... with political, technical, and commercial leadership.

These various definitions share the common assumption that competitiveness involves the ability to expand the sales of goods and services in international markets. This ability is conditioned by two factors:[1]

(i) Short-run macroeconomic factors: a lack of competitiveness is regarded as a problem with real exchange rates when a country in full employment runs a persistent and unwelcome current account deficit which will in due course require adjustment, usually via a mixture of deflation and depreciation (Boltho, 1996, p.2). The measures of competitiveness here are the relative price and/or cost indices expressed in a common currency. Working on the assumption that the underlying common factors are constant (or irrelevant), this approach focuses on the types of short-term macroeconomic management which affect the relative prices of national goods and services relative to other countries.

---

[1] Lall (2001, p.1503).

(ii) Medium- and long-run structural factors: competitiveness is thought to be conditioned by factors such as productivity, innovation, skills, etc. (Fagerberg 1996). These factors are the focus of most analyses on national competitiveness.

4.2.2 Con's

Recent critics of the concept of international competitiveness have charged that the concept is invalid. While the widespread discussion of competitiveness may suggest that it has an accepted definition and measures, these detractors argue that this is not the case, at least in the science of economics. As Lall (2001) has pointed out, the concept was originally conceived as a basis for strategic analyses in business school literature. Companies compete in markets for goods and resources. They measure competitiveness using relative market shares or profitability and they implement competitiveness strategy to increase their performance.

National competitiveness is assumed to be similar. Economies compete with each other in international markets for goods and factors. They can measure competitive performance and design competitiveness policy accordingly. The "Con's" literature suggests that this may make sense for competitive performance in specific activities. An economist may argue, for example, that it is "meaningful" to say that the United States has become less competitive in making television sets or textiles and more competitive in making computers, whereas it may be "meaningless" to say that the United States is becoming less or more competitive as an economy.

Krugman (1994 p.44) typifies the Con's point of view when he states, "...competitiveness is a meaningless word when applied to national economies. And the obsession with competitiveness is both wrong and dangerous." As Krugman frames it, the people preoccupied with national competitiveness misunderstand simple economic theory, or even worse, understand but ignore it. His contentions raise two separate issues: (i) whether "national competitiveness" has a valid economic definition, and (ii) if it does, whether competitiveness strategy is justifiable.[2] Krugman also argues that the concept of national competitiveness and the associated structural factors mentioned above are in conflict with the basic theory of comparative advantage. When nations trade with each other, as opposed to firms, they do not engage in competitive collusion. Whereas a gain in market share for a competing firm will inevitably decrease the market share of at least one of its competitors, nations engage in a non-zero sum game that

[2] Lall (2001).

benefits all parties. With the gains they reap from specialization according to their factor endowments, all participating countries do better with trade than they would without it. Focusing on competitive gaps in particular activities is partial and misleading. Weakening competitiveness in a few sectors (e.g. televisions or textiles) does not imply that the US economy is becoming less competitive. Declines in the competitiveness of certain industries may reflect changes in the pattern of endowments and indicate a need to reallocate resources from old to new areas of comparative advantage. The only important condition in a general equilibrium setting is optimal resource allocation, not the rise or decline of particular activities. The finding and defining of national competitiveness would therefore be a daunting and meaningless task.

Nevertheless, the criticisms raised in the "Con's" literature do not necessarily exclude "competitiveness" as a valid issue in economics. As is well known in economic theory, the concept of comparative advantage is based on some assumptions and optimized resource allocation through free trade occurs only when several strong assumptions hold. These assumptions include perfect competition with efficient markets, homogenous products, universal access to technology with no learning costs, and no externalities. If those assumptions are not met, which is a closer case to the real world, competitiveness might become more "meaningful" as an economic concept. When there are market failures, resources are allocated at a sub-optimal level, therefore countries can improve their competitiveness and ultimately their resource allocations, by taking proactive actions. Such concept of competitiveness is particularly important for developing countries where market failures are striking. As Lall (2001) stresses, the main aim of competitiveness strategy in the context of market imperfections is to help countries realize or build dynamic advantages.

Porter (1990), a pioneer of the concept of national competitiveness, points out that a country cannot be "competitive in all industries." After reviewing various concepts of competitiveness ('every firm is competitive,' 'positive balance of trade,' 'market share,' 'job creation'), he even comes quite close to concluding that national competitiveness is meaningless in and of itself. "The search for a convincing explanation of both national and firm prosperity must begin by asking the right question," he emphasizes. "We must abandon the whole notion of a "competitive nation" as a term having much meaning for economic prosperity. The principle goal of a nation is to produce a high and rising standard of living for its citizens. The ability to do so depends not on the amorphous notion of competitiveness but on the productivity with which a nation's resources (labor and capital) are employed... The only meaningful concept of competitiveness at the national level is national productivity" (Porter, 1990). In commenting on Porter's analysis, Reich (1990) similarly dismisses national competitiveness as "one of the rare terms of public discourse that have gone directly from obscurity to meaninglessness without any intervening period of coherence."[3]

In this study we will analyze measures used to increase trade competitiveness, i.e. the ability to expand sales in the international market. Policymakers from developing countries have relied on exchange rate policy and productivity policy as key tools for achieving such goals. Here we will analyze the effectiveness of these two policy tools.

The devaluation of a local currency instantly reduces the prices of a country's exports in foreign currencies. On this basis, the devaluation is expected to raise the trade competitiveness of a country and boost exports immediately and automatically. Many developing countries will nominally devalue their currencies as a means of improving their trade competitiveness. When they do so, however, the resulting rise in domestic prices (including prices of imports and production factors) usually feeds into domestic inflation, creating an inflationary pressure which eventually spreads into the export sector over time. This inflationary effect in the export sector is somewhat stronger when the devaluating country is more dependent on the importation of the raw materials used in its export sector. As it turns out, many developing countries meet this condition. The inflation resulting as a side effect of the devaluation can offset the immediate gains in exports. In investigating the impact of exchange rate adjustment, one therefore has to correct the nominal exchange rate for any changes in domestic and foreign price levels. This results in a real exchange rate, the same rate used in many macroeconomic models. The policy tool, in contrast, is the nominal exchange rate. With the use of this tool, nominal devaluation will only improve trade competitiveness if it leads to real devaluation.[4]

Friedman (1953) assumes that nominal prices are set in the currencies of the producer countries and that the exchange rate changes will entirely pass through to the final users of the goods and alter prices at the export destination markets. Two assumptions underpin the concept of devaluation as a policy for instantly spurring competitiveness: (i) the prompt responsiveness of end consumer prices and (ii) the stickiness of producer prices. Both of these assumptions are controversial in the theoretical literature and often stand at odds with empirical findings.

The first assumption, "prompt responsiveness of end consumer prices," or what can be called "consumer-currency pricing," has been scrutinized and debated by groups such as Betts and Devereux (1996, 2000) and

[3] Aiginger (1998, p.161).

[4] Bahmani-Oskooee and Miteza (2002).

Chari, Kehoe and McGrattan (2000). We can quickly construct a theoretical model for this debate by remembering that actual physical goods often account for only a small share of the total price paid by the end consumer. The final price is considerably amplified by costs of transportation, distribution, non-traded marketing, retailing, and so on. When these costs exceed the actual cost for the physical goods, they reduce the effects of exchange rate devaluations on prices in export destination markets (McCallum and Nelson, 1999).

The second assumption, "stickiness of producer prices," has been sanctioned by Feldstein (1992) and Obstfeld and Rogoff (1995). Under this assumption, or what can be called "producer-currency pricing," we can draw three implications. (i) A flexible exchange rate policy leads to relative price adjustment: exchange rate flexibility substitutes for flexible nominal prices. (ii) The resulting flexible price allocation is a Pareto optimum: no monetary policy will lead to a more desirable allocation. (iii) This optimal policy is self-oriented: no policy coordination across countries is required or even desirable. Many reject the assumption of stickiness of producer prices. The principal reason for doing so is the pass-through mechanism from exchange rate to inflation: the depreciation of a local currency will increase the prices of imported consumption and intermediate goods, the price difference will be transmitted to the cost of production factors, and the prices of export goods will ultimately be inflated as a result. The inflationary effects of exchange rate devaluation have been explained in considerable detail in the literature.[5]

4.3 Empirical Techniques

4.3.1 Granger Causality Tests

In this section we empirically investigate the effectiveness of the exchange rate policy and productivity policy in bringing about stronger trade competitiveness. The pass-through mechanism from exchange rate to inflation is perhaps the most important issue to be analyzed when considering the exchange rate policy to promote international competitiveness. With this in mind, we employ various empirical techniques to verify such pass-through mechanism, or the causality between exchange rate and domestic inflation. We investigate both causality in mean and causality in variance, through three techniques: the Engle-Granger causality test, the Lag-Augmented-

[5] See, for example, Adams and Gros (1986) and Montiel and Ostry (1991).

VAR-based causality test, and the causality test based on the cross correlation function (CCF). To begin we will briefly explain each of these empirical techniques and subsequently we will present the results of our analyses based on those techniques

The Granger causality test, a tool proposed by Granger (1969) and popularized by Sims (1972), is based on a Vector Autoregression (VAR) or Vector Error Correction (VEC). Granger causality suggests that a variable Y_2 Granger causes a variable Y_1 if the former can help to build a more accurate forecast of the latter. The test proceeds as follows.

First, we test the stationarity of all variables by unit root test. If the variables are found to be non-stationary, we test for cointegration. When the null hypothesis of no-cointegration cannot be rejected, we estimate VAR formulated in first difference. As the present analysis considers a bivariate system, we can write the VAR as follows:

$$\Delta Y_{1t} = \phi_{10} + \sum_{k=1}^{p} \phi_{11}(k)\Delta Y_{1t-k} + \sum_{k=1}^{p} \phi_{12}(k)\Delta Y_{2t-k} + u_{1t}, \tag{4.1}$$

$$\Delta Y_{2t} = \phi_{20} + \sum_{k=1}^{p} \phi_{21}(k)\Delta Y_{1t-k} + \sum_{k=1}^{p} \phi_{22}(k)\Delta Y_{2t-k} + u_{2t}, \tag{4.2}$$

where Y_{1t} is the level of the price index at time t; Y_{2t} is the level of the exchange rate at time t; Δ represents first differences; ϕ_{10}, ϕ_{20}, ϕ_{11}, ϕ_{12}, ϕ_{21}, ϕ_{22} are parameters or vectors of parameters; u_{1t} and u_{2t} are error terms; and p is the lag length.

We test the hypothesis that Y_2 Granger causes Y_1 by testing the restrictions which set the coefficients $\phi_{12}(k)$ $(k = 1, 2, \cdots, p)$ to zero. Similarly, we test the hypothesis that Y_1 Granger causes Y_2 by testing the restrictions which set the coefficients $\phi_{21}(k)$ $(k = 1, 2, \cdots, p)$ to zero. Under the null hypothesis, the Wald statistic follows a Chi-square distribution with a degree of freedom equal to the number of excluded lagged variables.

When the null hypothesis of no-cointegration is rejected, we construct the following VEC:

$$\Delta Y_{1t} = \Gamma_{10} + \sum_{k=1}^{p} \Gamma_{11}(k)\Delta Y_{1t-k} + \sum_{k=1}^{p} \Gamma_{12}(k)\Delta Y_{2t-k} + \alpha_{10} EC_{t-1} + u_{1t}, \tag{4.3}$$

$$\Delta Y_{2t} = \Gamma_{20} + \sum_{k=1}^{p} \Gamma_{21}(k)\Delta Y_{1t-k} + \sum_{k=1}^{p} \Gamma_{22}(k)\Delta Y_{2t-k} + \alpha_{20} EC_{t-1} + u_{2t}, \tag{4.4}$$

where $\Gamma_{10}, \Gamma_{20}, \Gamma_{11}, \Gamma_{12}, \Gamma_{21}, \Gamma_{22}, \alpha_{10}, \alpha_{20}$ are parameters and EC_{t-1} is an error correction term derived from the cointegrating relation. Causality can be put forward in two ways in a VEC framework. First, the presence of cointegration indicates in itself causality, or a long-run interdependence between the variables; the direction can be determined theoretically or intuitively. Second, we can inspect short-run causality using lagged parameters restrictions tests, as in the VAR. Namely, Y_2 causes Y_1 in the short run if the null hypothesis of $\Gamma_{12}(k) = 0$ $(k = 1, ..., p)$ is rejected, and similarly Y_1 causes Y_2 in the short run if the null hypothesis of $\Gamma_{21}(k) = 0$ $(k = 1, ..., p)$ is rejected. As for the VAR, the Wald statistic under the null hypothesis follows a Chi-square distribution with a degree of freedom equal to the number of excluded lagged variables.

4.3.2 LA-VAR Causality Tests

Here we will attempt to ascertain the accuracy of the results of the VAR and VEC-based Granger causality test using the "Lag-Augmented-VAR-based causality test." The LA-VAR technique, developed by Toda and Yamamoto (1995), allows the testing of coefficient restrictions in a level VAR when the variables are of unknown integration or cointegration order. As mentioned above, the construction of the usual VAR or VEC relies on the prior test of integration or cointegration order. It has been pointed out, however, that the conclusions of the two tests might be debatable, especially when testing with small sample sizes. If there are indeed flaws in these conclusions, the coefficient restrictions test based on the usual VAR or VEC will presumably be subject to pretest biases. The LA-VAR method eludes these biases by elaborating the Granger causality test and other tests of coefficient restriction, i.e. tests which are robust to the arbitrary integration and cointegration order of the variables.

The method proceeds, briefly, as follows. Let $\{y_t\}$, the n-dimensional vector constituted by the level of the variables in the study, be generated by:

$$y_t = g_0 + g_1 t + J_1 y_{t-1} + J_2 y_{t-2} + ... + J_k y_{t-k} + e_t, \quad t = 1, 2, ...T, \qquad (4.5)$$

where t represents the time trend, k, the lag length, $g_0, g_1, J_1, J_2, ..., J_k$, the vectors or matrices of coefficients, and ε_t, an i.i.d sequence of n-dimensional random vectors with zero mean and covariance matrix Σ_ε.

Suppose the interest is on testing restrictions on a subset of parameters in the model, formulated as:

$$H_0 : f(\phi) = 0 . \tag{4.6}$$

The test can be conducted through the following VAR model, in level form, estimated by Ordinary Least Squares (OLS):

$$y_t = \hat{\gamma}_0 + \hat{\gamma}_1 t + \hat{J}_1 y_{t-1} + \hat{J}_2 y_{t-2} + \ldots + \hat{J}_p y_{t-p} + \hat{\varepsilon}_t , \tag{4.7}$$

where circumflex (^) indicates an estimation by OLS and $p \geq k + d_{max}$ represents the true lag length k augmented by a suspected maximum integration order d_{max} ($k \geq d_{max}$). Since the true values of $J_{k+1}, \ldots, J_p$ are zero, those parameters are not included in restriction (4.6). Toda and Yamamoto establish that if $p \geq k + d_{max}$ under the null hypothesis in (4.6), the Wald statistic will asymptotically follow a Chi-square distribution with the degrees of freedom equal to the number of excluded lagged variables regardless of the integration order of the process or the existence of a cointegrating relation.

4.3.3 Cross Correlation Function Approach

The CCF approach can be explained using the models presented by Cheung and Ng (1996) and Hamori (2003). As with the previous causality tests, the CCF approach on causality suggests that a series of values Y_1, grouped together as a set of information, will cause Y_2 if it helps to build a more accurate forecast of the latter. The technique consists of a two-step causality test which remains asymptotically robust to distributional assumptions.

The first step is to estimate a univariate time-series model for each of the variables, in order to allow for time variation in both conditional means and conditional variances. The second step is to construct two types of new time series: the resulting residuals standardized by conditional variances and the squares of the standardized residuals. Next, the CCF of the standardized residuals of two series is examined to test for causality in mean. Once this is accomplished, the CCF of the squares of the standardized residuals of the two series is investigated to test for causality in variance.

We assume that Y_1 and Y_2 can be expressed as:

$$Y_{1t} = \mu_{y_1,t} + \sqrt{h_{y_1,t}}\varepsilon_t, \tag{4.8}$$

$$Y_{2t} = \mu_{y_2,t} + \sqrt{h_{y_2,t}}\zeta_t, \tag{4.9}$$

where $\mu_{y_1,t}$ and $\mu_{y_2,t}$ are the mean values of Y_1 and Y_2, $h_{y_1,t}$ and $h_{y_2,t}$ are variances of the error terms, and $\{\varepsilon_t\}$ and $\{\zeta_t\}$ are independent white noise processes with zero mean and unit variance.

Estimates of the following standardized residuals are used to test the causality in mean:

$$\varepsilon_t = \frac{Y_{1t} - \mu_{y_1,t}}{\sqrt{h_{y_1,t}}}, \tag{4.10}$$

$$\zeta_t = \frac{Y_{2t} - \mu_{y_2,t}}{\sqrt{h_{y_2,t}}}. \tag{4.11}$$

The sample correlation coefficient at lag k is computed from consistent estimates of the conditional mean and variance of Y_{1t} and Y_{2t}, as follows:

$$\widehat{\gamma}_{\varepsilon\zeta}(k) = \frac{c_{\varepsilon\zeta}(k)}{\sqrt{c_{\varepsilon\varepsilon}(0)c_{\zeta\zeta}(0)}}, \tag{4.12}$$

where $c_{\varepsilon\zeta}(k)$ is the $k-$th lag sample cross-covariance given by

$$c_{\varepsilon\zeta}(k) = \frac{1}{T}\sum(\widehat{\varepsilon}_t - \overline{\widehat{\varepsilon}})(\widehat{\zeta}_{t-k} - \overline{\widehat{\zeta}}), \quad k = 0, \pm1, \pm2, \ldots, \tag{4.13}$$

and $c_{\varepsilon\varepsilon}(0)$ and $c_{\zeta\zeta}(0)$ are the respective sample variances of ε_t and ζ_t.

The null hypothesis of no causality in mean can be tested using $\sqrt{T}(\widehat{\gamma}_{\varepsilon\zeta}(k_1),\ldots,\widehat{\gamma}_{\varepsilon\zeta}(k_m))$, which converges in distribution to $N(0, I_m)$. The test of causality at a specified lag k can be carried out using the statistic $\sqrt{T}\widehat{\gamma}_{\varepsilon\zeta}(k)$ and the standard normal distribution. A test statistic larger than the critical value of normal distribution implies a rejection of the null of no causality in mean.

Next, the estimated values of the following squared standardized residuals are used to test the causality in variance:

$$u_t = \frac{(Y_{1t} - \mu_{y_1,t})^2}{h_{y_1,t}} = \varepsilon_t^2, \tag{4.14}$$

$$v_t = \frac{(Y_{2t} - \mu_{y_2,t})^2}{h_{y_2,t}} = \zeta_t^2. \tag{4.15}$$

The sample correlation coefficient at lag k is computed from consistent estimates of the conditional mean and variance of Y_{1t} and Y_{2t}, as follows:

$$\widehat{\gamma}_{uv}(k) = \frac{c_{uv}(k)}{\sqrt{c_{uu}(0)c_{vv}(0)}}, \tag{4.16}$$

where $c_{uv}(k)$ is the $k-$ th lag sample cross-covariance given by

$$c_{uv}(k) = \frac{1}{T}\sum(\widehat{u}_t - \overline{\widehat{u}})(\widehat{v}_{t-k} - \overline{\widehat{v}}), \quad k = 0, \pm 1, \pm 2, \ldots, \tag{4.17}$$

and $c_{uu}(0)$ and $c_{vv}(0)$ are the respective sample variances of u_t and v_t.

The null hypothesis of no causality in variance can be tested using $\sqrt{T}(\widehat{\gamma}_{uv}(k_1), \ldots, \widehat{\gamma}_{uv}(k_m))$, which converges in distribution to $N(0, I_m)$. The test of causality at a specified lag k can be carried out using the statistic $\sqrt{T}\widehat{\gamma}_{uv}(k)$ and the standard normal distribution. A test statistic larger than the critical value of normal distribution implies a rejection of the null of no causality in variance.

The CCF approach is employed to re-examine the causality in mean and to investigate causality in variance between the exchange rate and the price index. The list of countries, the data used, and the sample period are similar to those of the two previous causality tests.

In the first step, as explained above, we estimate univariate models following the AR(k)-EGARCH(p, q) specification. EGARCH is the exponential generalized autoregressive conditionally heteroskedasticity model, developed by Nelson (1991). We can write the conditional mean and conditional variance as follows:

$$y_t = \pi_0 + \sum_{i=1}^{k} \pi_i y_{t-i} + \varepsilon_t, \tag{4.18}$$

$$\log(\sigma_t^2) = \omega + \sum_{i=1}^{q} \beta_i \log(\sigma_{t-i}^2) + \sum_{i=1}^{p} \alpha_i \left| \frac{\varepsilon_{t-i}}{\sigma_{t-i}} \right| + \sum_{i=1}^{p} \gamma_i \frac{\varepsilon_{t-i}}{\sigma_{t-i}}. \qquad (4.19)$$

Each equation is estimated by Maximum Likelihood. Next, we use the method proposed by Bollerslev and Wooldridge (1992) to compute the asymptotic standard errors, which are robust to departures from normality. Based on SBIC and the diagnostic test, we choose k from 1 to 4, q from 1 and 2, and p from 1 and 2. Table 4.3 lists the specifications of the univariate models for the exchange rates and price indexes of every country.[6]

In the second step, we collect the standardized residuals from the previously estimated AR(k)-EGARCH(p,q) models into time-series. We compute the cross correlation coefficients between the residuals of the exchange rate and the residuals of the price index using the procedure described above. We then obtain the test statistic by multiplying the cross correlation coefficient at a specific lag with the square root of the number of observations, and apply the standard normal distribution. Using the lag and lead patterns of causality provided by this technique, we focus on the correlation coefficients between lags of the exchange rate and the current values of the price index. In other words, we focus on cases where the price index lags behind exchange rates, as this allows us to examine causality from the latter to the former.

4.4 Data

Here we apply the VAR-based Granger causality test to analyze the pass-through mechanism from exchange rate to inflation The analysis is performed using monthly data from January 1960 to April 2004[7] on 27 economies from sub-Saharan Africa (all of the economies in sub-Saharan Africa with available data), 8 selected economies from Latin America, and 5 selected economies from East and Southeast Asia. Data were taken from the International Financial Statistics (International Monetary Fund, June 2004). The exchange rate is measured as local currency per unit of US Dollar. The consumer price index (base year 1995) is used as the price index.

---

[6] We omit the estimated models to save space.

[7] The sample spans are shorter for economies where data for the full sample are not available.

4.5 Empirical Results

The Engle–Granger cointegration test is carried out for pairs of variables in each country. The results are presented in Column 2 of Table 4.1. We find evidence of cointegration between the exchange rate and CPI in only 5 of the countries. Accordingly, we run the Granger causality test based on VEC for the 5 countries where cointegration is found and based on the usual VAR for the other 35 countries. The results of the causality test are presented in Columns 3 and 4 of Table 4.1. If we accept the aforementioned assumption that the causality relationship arises from both the cointegration relationship and causality test, we find causality from the exchange rate to CPI in 33 out of the 40 countries. In other words, exchange rate depreciation will feed into the price level to bring about high inflation. The inflation equation presented above is verified. The higher price levels, in combination with the higher wage and production costs they elicit (explained in the theoretical model), will push up the prices of home goods (some of which are exported). Hence, the assumption of fixed producer prices, the core rationale behind the devaluation policy to strengthen competitiveness, might not hold.

Then, we apply the LA-VAR-based causality test to re-examine the pass-through mechanism from the exchange rate to inflation. The data and sample period are similar to those used in the VAR-based causality test. The results are given in Table 4.2. The pass-through mechanism from the exchange rate to CPI is found in 35 out of the 40 countries of our sample. Causality from the exchange rate to the price index is identified in 24 out of the 27 sub-Saharan African economies in our sample.

Table 4.1. Engle-Granger cointegration and VAR- and VEC-based causality tests from exchange rate to price index

Country	Cointegration Test[(a)]	Causality Test[(b)]	p-value[(c)]
Africa			
Benin	–1.876	1.609	0.100
Botswana	–2.031	1.047	0.406
Burkina Faso	–2.093	2.131	0.049
Burundi	–2.472	3.189	0.042
Cameroon	–1.853	2.559	0.003
Chad	–2.651	4.199	0.000
Congo, Dem. Rep.	–2.478	1.836	0.040
Côte d'Ivoire	–1.739	3.142	0.044
Gabon	–1.575	3.851	0.000
Gambia	–1.678	2.570	0.003
Ghana	–1.762	0.681	0.770

Table 4.1. (cont.)

Country	Cointegration Test[(a)]	Causality Test[(b)]	p-value[(c)]
Guinea-Bissau	–3.874**	40.256	0.000
Kenya	–2.290	3.218	0.000
Madagascar	–2.029	3.519	0.000
Malawi	–2.659	2.618	0.003
Mali	–2.412	2.316	0.035
Mauritius	–2.047	2.260	0.037
Mozambique	–2.707	3.606	0.000
Nigeria	–1.678	1.398	0.163
Rwanda	–1.176	1.972	0.025
Senegal	–1.990	2.366	0.006
Sierra Leone	–4.359***	6.682	0.351
South Africa	–1.939	3.910	0.000
Swaziland	–1.996	0.666	0.784
Togo	–2.668	4.792	0.000
Zambia	–3.033*	21.429	0.006
Zimbabwe	–1.143	2.333	0.099
Asia			
Korea, Rep.	–2.143	2.674	0.002
Philippines	–3.048*	10.978	0.089
Malaysia	–0.764	0.929	0.518
Thailand	–1.976	0.604	0.839
Indonesia	–2.368	6.852	0.000
Latin America			
Brazil	–15.246***	5.458	0.000
Mexico	–2.132	7.572	0.000
Bolivia	–2.418	13.504	0.000
Colombia	–1.248	5.239	0.000
Costa Rica	–2.461	12.492	0.000
Dominican Rep.	–2.206	1.941	0.073
Ecuador	–1.555	4.354	0.000
Venezuela, RB	–2.300	2.744	0.001

Notes:
(a): values indicate the ADF-statistic of the unit root test on residuals of the cointegration equation
(b): values indicate the F-statistic of causality test based on VAR or VEC
(c): p-values corresponding to the F-statistic of causality test
***, (**), and [*] indicate significance at 1%, (5%), and [10%].

Table 4.2. LA-VAR-based causality test on exchange rate and price index

Country	True Lag Length	F-stat[a]	p-value[b]
Africa			
Benin	6	3.048	0.008
Botswana	9	0.785	0.582
Burkina Faso	6	1.937	0.073
Burundi	6	1.756	0.100
Cameroon	6	3.571	0.002
Chad	6	7.447	0.000
Congo, Dem. Rep.	6	2.139	0.048
Côte d'Ivoire	2	2.768	0.064
Gabon	6	6.452	0.000
Gambia	8	2.722	0.006
Ghana	6	0.493	0.814
Guinea-Bissau	6	4.590	0.000
Kenya	8	4.612	0.000
Madagascar	6	6.250	0.000
Malawi	12	2.961	0.001
Mali	8	2.662	0.009
Mauritius	6	2.069	0.055
Mozambique	6	4.550	0.000
Nigeria	12	1.598	0.089
Rwanda	12	1.937	0.029
Senegal	6	2.963	0.008
Sierra Leone	6	2.417	0.029
South Africa	12	3.094	0.000
Swaziland	9	0.581	0.746
Togo	6	6.199	0.000
Zambia	8	1.927	0.058
Zimbabwe	2	2.383	0.094
Asia			
Korea, Rep.	6	3.030	0.007
Philippines	6	2.437	0.025
Malaysia	6	0.895	0.499
Thailand	8	0.405	0.918
Indonesia	8	8.653	0.000
Latin America			
Brazil	8	8.162	0.000
Mexico	6	12.910	0.000
Bolivia	12	14.201	0.000
Colombia	12	5.121	0.000

Table 4.2. (cont.)

Country	True Lag Length	F-stat[(a)]	p-value[(b)]
Costa Rica	12	11.204	0.000
Dominican Rep.	6	2.005	0.064
Ecuador	6	9.007	0.000
Venezuela, RB	6	2.903	0.009

Notes:
(a): values indicate the F-statistic of causality test based on LA-VAR.
(b): p-values corresponding to the F-statistic of causality test.

The LA-VAR-based causality technique confirms the findings from the VAR or VEC-based causality test, i.e. that the exchange rate devaluation brings about higher inflation in the domestic economy and thereby might offset the expected effect on export competitiveness.

Finally, we employ the third technique, the Cross Correlation Function (CCF), to (i) verify the robustness of the previous findings on mean causality and (ii) examine the variance causality. The full results, the lead and lag structures for residuals and squared residuals of 40 countries, are too voluminous to present here. Table 4.3 indicates the empirical model of the consumer price index and the exchange rate for each country. Table 4.4 summarizes the existence or non-existence of causality in mean and variance for each country, based on the CCF approach. When one or more correlation coefficients at a specific lag are statistically significant at the 10% significance level or better, we conclude that a causality relationship from the exchange rate to the price index exists.

Causality in mean from the exchange rate to the price index is confirmed to exist in 36 out of the 40 countries examined. Causality in mean is confirmed to exist in 26 of the 27 countries of sub-Saharan Africa. Interestingly, our method confirms the existence of causality in variance from the exchange rate to the price index in more than two-thirds of the sample countries. Causality in variance is confirmed in 19 of the 27 countries of sub-Saharan Africa.

Table 4.3. AR-EGARCH model specification of exchange rate and price index

Country	Variable[(a)]	Specification	SBIC
Africa			
Benin	CPI	AR(1)-EGARCH(1,1)	–5.400
	EXC	AR(2)-EGARCH(1,2)	–5.216
Botswana	CPI	AR(2)-EGARCH(1,4)	–7.556
	EXC	AR(2)-EGARCH(1,1)	–5.938
Burkina Faso	CPI	AR(1)-EGARCH(1,1)	–4.599
	EXC	AR(2)-EGARCH(1,2)	–5.216
Burundi	CPI	AR(2)-EGARCH(2,2)	–4.799
	EXC	AR(2)-EGARCH(1,4)	–5.608

Table 4.3. (cont.)

Country	Variable[(a)]	Specification	SBIC
Cameroon	CPI	AR(2)-EGARCH(2,3)	–5.625
	EXC	AR(2)-EGARCH(1,2)	–5.216
Chad	CPI	AR(1)-EGARCH(1,1)	–4.393
	EXC	AR(2)-EGARCH(1,3)	–5.148
Congo, Dem. Rep.	CPI	AR(2)-EGARCH(2,1)	–2.267
	EXC	AR(2)-EGARCH(1,4)	–2.542
Côte d'Ivoire	CPI	AR(2)-EGARCH(2,3)	–5.369
	EXC	AR(2)-EGARCH(1,2)	–5.216
Gabon	CPI	AR(2)-EGARCH(2,3)	–5.840
	EXC	AR(2)-EGARCH(1,2)	–5.216
Gambia	CPI	AR(2)-EGARCH(2,4)	–4.964
	EXC	AR(2)-EGARCH(1,1)	–5.377
Ghana	CPI	AR(2)-EGARCH(2,4)	–4.751
	EXC	AR(2)-EGARCH(2,1)	–4.862
Guinea-Bissau	CPI	AR(2)-EGARCH(1,4)	–3.290
	EXC	AR(2)-EGARCH(1,2)	–4.405
Kenya	CPI	AR(1)-EGARCH(1,3)	–5.953
	EXC	AR(2)-EGARCH(2,4)	–6.249
Madagascar	CPI	AR(2)-EGARCH(2,4)	–5.770
	EXC	AR(2)-EGARCH(1,3)	–5.948
Malawi	CPI	AR(2)-EGARCH(2,4)	–4.782
	EXC	AR(2)-EGARCH(1,1)	–5.288
Mali	CPI	AR(1)-EGARCH(2,1)	–6.187
	EXC	AR(2)-EGARCH(2,2)	–5.252
Mauritius	CPI	AR(1)-EGARCH(1,2)	–6.396
	EXC	AR(2)-EGARCH(1,1)	–6.203
Mozambique	CPI	AR(2)-EGARCH(2,3)	–5.380
	EXC	AR(2)-EGARCH(2,4)	–5.546
Nigeria	CPI	AR(2)-EGARCH(2,4)	–5.256
	EXC	AR(2)-EGARCH(2,1)	–4.441
Rwanda	CPI	AR(2)-EGARCH(2,2)	–5.636
	EXC	AR(2)-EGARCH(2,4)	–4.860
Senegal	CPI	AR(1)-EGARCH(1,3)	–5.347
	EXC	AR(2)-EGARCH(1,3)	–5.148
Sierra Leone	CPI	AR(1)-EGARCH(2,3)	–3.261
	EXC	AR(2)-EGARCH(2,3)	–4.463
South Africa	CPI	AR(2)-EGARCH(1,4)	–8.068
	EXC	AR(2)-EGARCH(1,4)	–5.905
Swaziland	CPI	AR(2)-EGARCH(2,4)	–5.641
	EXC	AR(2)-EGARCH(1,3)	–5.909
Togo	CPI	AR(1)-EGARCH(2,1)	–5.055
	EXC	AR(2)-EGARCH(1,1)	–5.181
Zambia	CPI	AR(2)-EGARCH(1,3)	–4.686
	EXC	AR(1)-EGARCH(1,3)	–4.350

Table 4.3. (cont.)

Country	Variable[a]	Specification	SBIC
Zimbabwe	CPI	AR(2)-EGARCH(2,3)	–5.436
	EXC	AR(2)-EGARCH(2,2)	–3.880
Asia			
Korea, Rep.	CPI	AR(1)-EGARCH(1,4)	–7.544
	EXC	AR(2)-EGARCH(2,3)	–5.904
Philippines	CPI	AR(2)-EGARCH(2,3)	–6.770
	EXC	AR(2)-EGARCH(1,3)	–5.985
Malaysia	CPI	AR(2)-EGARCH(2,4)	–8.063
	EXC	AR(2)-EGARCH(2,4)	–6.402
Thailand	CPI	AR(1)-EGARCH(1,3)	–7.790
	EXC	AR(2)-EGARCH(2,4)	–8.829
Indonesia	CPI	AR(2)-EGARCH(2,4)	2.530
	EXC	AR(1)-EGARCH(2,4)	–4.828
Latin America			
Brazil	CPI	AR(1)-EGARCH(2,2)	–5.601
	EXC	AR(2)-EGARCH(2,4)	–2.472
Mexico	CPI	AR(2)-EGARCH(2,4)	–5.426
	EXC	AR(2)-EGARCH(2,3)	–6.689
Bolivia	CPI	AR(1)-EGARCH(2,4)	–5.095
	EXC	AR(2)-EGARCH(1,4)	–4.535
Colombia	CPI	AR(1)-EGARCH(1,4)	–7.103
	EXC	AR(2)-EGARCH(1,4)	–7.111
Costa Rica	CPI	AR(2)-EGARCH(1,4)	–6.677
	EXC	AR(2)-EGARCH(2,4)	–8.038
Dominican Rep.	CPI	AR(1)-EGARCH(1,4)	–5.682
	EXC	AR(2)-EGARCH(2,4)	–7.360
Ecuador	CPI	AR(2)-EGARCH(2,2)	–5.922
	EXC	AR(2)-EGARCH(2,2)	–6.033
Venezuela, RB	CPI	AR(1)-EGARCH(2,4)	–7.050
	EXC	AR(1)-EGARCH(1,4)	–5.068

Notes:
(a): CPI indicates the consumer price index, and EXC shows the exchange rate.

Table 4.4. CCF approach: mean and variance causality from exchange rate to price index

Country	Causality in Mean From EXC to CPI	Causality in Variance From EXC to CPI
Africa		
Benin	O	X
Botswana	O	O
Burkina Faso	O	O
Burundi	O	O
Cameroon	O	O

Table 4.4. (cont.)

Country	Causality in Mean From EXC to CPI	Causality in Variance From EXC to CPI
Chad	O	O
Congo, Dem. Rep.	O	X
Côte d'Ivoire	O	O
Gabon	O	O
Gambia	O	O
Ghana	X	X
Guinea-Bissau	O	X
Kenya	O	O
Madagascar	O	O
Malawi	O	O
Mali	O	O
Mauritius	O	X
Mozambique	O	O
Nigeria	O	X
Rwanda	O	O
Senegal	O	X
Sierra Leone	O	O
South Africa	O	O
Swaziland	O	O
Togo	O	X
Zambia	O	O
Zimbabwe	O	O
Asia		
Korea, Rep.	O	O
Philippines	O	O
Malaysia	O	O
Thailand	O	O
Indonesia	O	O
Latin America		
Brazil	O	O
Mexico	O	O
Bolivia	X	X
Colombia	O	O
Costa Rica	O	O
Dominican Rep.	X	X
Ecuador	X	O
Venezuela, RB	O	O

Notes:
O indicates the existence of causality.
X indicates the non-existence of causality.

4.6 Conclusion

In sum, we can recapitulate the results from the three techniques as follows (Table 4.5):

- Results for the entire sample (40 countries):

Causality in mean from the exchange rate to the price index is found in 39 countries, based on at least one of the three techniques used in this study (the VAR-based Granger causality test, the LA-VAR-based causality test, or the causality test based on the CCF approach). Ghana is the only country without evidence of causality.

Causality in mean from the exchange rate to the price index is confirmed by all three techniques in 31 countries. Causality in variance from the exchange rate to the price index is found in 30 countries. Causality from the exchange rate to the price index is found in 39 countries using at least one of four techniques. Ghana is the only country without evidence of causality in either mean or in variance.

Table 4.5. Recapitulation, causality from exchange rate to CPI

		Full sample (40 countries)	Sub-Saharan Africa (27 countries)
Mean Causality	VAR - VEC	33 countries	22 countries
	LA - VAR	35 countries	24 countries
	CCF	36 countries	26 countries
	All three techniques	30 countries	22 countries
	At least one of the three techniques	39 countries	26 countries
Variance Causality	CCF	30 countries	19 countries
Either Mean or Variance Causality	At least one of the three Techniques	39 countries	26 countries

Note: This table lists the numbers of countries with confirmed causality from Exchange Rate to CPI.

- Results for the sub-Saharan African economies (27 countries):

Causality in mean from the exchange rate to the price index is found in 26 countries, based on at least one of the three techniques used in this study (the VAR-based Granger causality test, the LA-VAR-based causality test, or the causality test based on the CCF approach).

Causality in mean from the exchange rate to the price index is confirmed by all three techniques in 23 countries. Causality in variance from the exchange rate to the price index is found in 19 countries. Causality from the exchange rate to the price index is found in 26 countries using at least one of four techniques.

Thus, the assumption that the producer price is fixed, the rationale behind the use of the exchange rate policy to strengthen international competitiveness, does not hold in most of the countries examined in this analysis. Depreciation of the local currency drives up inflation, wages, and production costs, which in turn increases the prices of home goods denominated in the local currency and might thereby offset the expected gains in international competitiveness. In the next section we investigate the potential for this adverse outcome by directly analyzing the relationship between the exchange rate and export price index.

References

Adams, C. and Gros, D. (1986) Consequences of real exchange rate rules for inflation: Some illustrative examples, *IMF Staff Papers,* **33**, 439-76.

Aiginger, K. (1998) A framework for evaluating the dynamic competitiveness of countries, *Structural Change and Economic Dynamics,* **9**, 159-188.

Bahmani-Oskooee, M. and Miteza, I. (2002) Do nominal devaluations lead to real devaluations in LDCs? *Economics Letters*, **74**, 385-391.

Betts, C. and Devereux, M. (1996) The exchange rate in a model of pricing-to-market, *European Economic Review*, **40**, 1007-1021.

Betts, C. and Devereux, M. (2000) Exchange rate dynamics in a model of pricing-to-market, *Journal of International Economics*, **50**, 215-224.

Bollerslev, T. and Wooldridge, J. (1992) Quasi-maximum likelihood estimation and inference in dynamic models with time varying covariances, *Econometric Reviews*, **11**, 143-172.

Boltho, A. (1996) International competitiveness, *Oxford Review of Economic Policy*, **12**, 1-96.

Chari, V.V., Kehoe, P.J. and McGrattan, E.R. (2000) Sticky price models of the business cycle: can the contract multiplier solve the persistence problem? *Econometrica*, **68**, 1151-79.

Cheung, Y.-W., and Ng, L.K. (1996), A causality-in-variance test and its application to financial market prices, *Journal of Econometrics*, **72**, 33-48.

Competitiveness Policy Council (1994) *Promoting Long-Term Prosperity: Third Report to the President & Congress*, U.S. Government Printing Office, Washington, D.C.

Fagerberg, J. (1988) International competitiveness, *Economic Journal*, **98**, 355-74.

Fagerberg, J. (1996) Technology and competitiveness, *Oxford Review of Economic Policy*, **12**, 39-51.

Feldstein, M. (1992) The case against the EMU, *The Economist*, (June 13th, 1992), 19-22

Friedman, M. (1953) The case for flexible exchange rates, in *Essays in Positive Economics*, University of Chicago Press, Chicago, 157-203

Granger, C.W.J. (1969) Investigating causal relations by econometric models and cross-spectral methods, *Econometrica*, **34**, 161-194.

Hamori, S. (2003) *An Empirical Investigation of Stock Market: The CCF Approach*, Kluwer Academic Publishers, Dordrecht.

Krugman, P. (1994) Competitiveness: a dangerous obsession, *Foreign Affairs*, **73**, 28-44

Lall, S. (2001) Competitiveness indices and developing countries: An economic evaluation of the global competitiveness report, *World Development*, **29**, 1501-1525.

McCallum, B.T. and Nelson, E. (1999) An optimizing IS-LM specification for monetary policy and business cycle analysis, *Journal of Money, Credit and Banking*, **31**, 296-316.

Montiel, P. J. and Ostry, J.D. (1991) Macro implications of real exchange rate targeting in developing countries, *IMF Staff Papers*, **38**, 872-900.

Nelson, D.B. (1991) Conditional heteroskedasticity in asset returns: a new approach, *Econometrica*, **59**, 347-370.

OECD (1995a) *Competitiveness Policy: A New Agenda*, DSTI/IND (95) **14**, Paris.

OECD (1995b) *Competitiveness: An Overview of Reports Issued in Member Countries*, DSTI/IND (95) **15**, Paris.

OECD/TEP (1992) *Technology and the Economy, The Key Relationships*, The Technology/Economy Programme, Paris.

Obstfeld, M. and Rogoff, K. (1995) The mirage of fixed exchange rates, *Journal of Economic Perspectives*, **9**, 73-96.

Porter M.E. (1990) *The Competitive Advantage of Nations*, Free Press, New York.

Reich, R. (1990) But now we're global, *The Times Literary Supplement*, **31**, 925-26.

Scott, B.R. and Lodge, G.C. ed., (1985) *US Competitiveness and the World Economy*, Harvard Business School Press, Boston, MA.

Sims, C.A. (1972) Money, income and causality, *American Economic Review*, **62**, 540-552.

Toda, H.Y. and Yamamoto, T. (1995) Statistical inference in vector autoregressions with possibly integrated processes, *Journal of Econometrics*, **66**, 225-250.

5 Trade Competitiveness: Exchange Rate, Productivity, and Export Price

5.1 Introduction

This chapter empirically investigates the effectiveness of the exchange rate policy and productivity policy in strengthening trade competitiveness.

As we learned in the last chapter, causality from the exchange rate to the price index is confirmed in almost all of the countries examined (39 of 40). Henceforth we will examine whether the pass-through mechanism offsets the expected effects of devaluation policy on competitiveness. Various measures of international competitiveness have been proposed in the literature. Many studies use the real exchange rate, while others use the real effective exchange rate, an alternative which considers factors such as domestic and foreign inflation. Given our fairly narrow focus of interest here, the ability of the countries to sell in international markets, we use the price index of the exports of each country as a measure of competitiveness. This index allows us to directly quantify increases or decreases in a country's competitiveness relative to the previous year[1]. In selecting any measure, we must remember that the adverse effects of the exchange rate on export price might arise only after the short-run impacts of the previously studied causality. We account for this by adopting an empirical technique, cointegration analysis, to analyze the long-term relationship. If devaluation policy ultimately strengthens competitiveness in the medium- and long-run, we can expect cointegration of the exchange rate and export price; when no cointegration relationship is found, the beneficial effects of the devaluation policy might be offset by the resulting accumulated inflation.

---

[1] Note, however, that this index only compares the country to itself. Thus, it omits changes of competitiveness of other countries exporting to the same international markets. These types of studies require more comprehensive analyses.

This chapter also analyzes productivity policy, the second policy customarily adopted to strengthen trade competitiveness. Productivity policy is premised on the notion that higher productivity of production factors, i.e. capital and labor, ultimately brings down the prices of goods produced domestically, including export goods, by decreasing the unit production cost. Lower prices of domestically produced goods for exports strengthen a country's competitiveness in international trade.

5.2 Empirical Techniques: "Bounds" Cointegration Tests

We adopt the "bounds test" of cointegration proposed by Pesaran et al. (2001). When working with a relatively small sample size, as in the present case, the accuracy of the results of unit root and cointegration tests often remains disputable. The bounds test permits a cointegration analysis irrespective of whether the variables are I(0) or I(1). This test produces more accurate estimates for small sample sizes than the usual residuals-based Engle-Granger test (Engle and Granger, 1987) or the VAR-based Johansen test (Johansen and Juselius, 1990).[2]

The bounds test starts from the estimation of an unrestricted error correction model (UECM) of the form

$$\begin{aligned}\Delta \ln Y_{2t} = \beta_0 + \sum_{i=0}^{k_1} \beta_{1i} \Delta \ln Y_{1t-i} + \sum_{i=0}^{k_2} \beta_{2i} \Delta \ln Y_{2t-i} \\ + \beta_3 \ln Y_{2t-1} + \beta_4 \ln Y_{1t-1} + u_{2t},\end{aligned} \tag{5.1}$$

where Δ and $\ln$ denote the first difference and logarithm, respectively. The bounds test methodology calls for an analysis of the null hypothesis of no cointegration through a joint significance test of the lagged variables $\ln Y_{2t-1}$ and $\ln Y_{1t-1}$ based on the Wald or F-statistic. Thus, the null hypothesis (H_0) and the alternative hypothesis (H_A) are given by,

$$H_0 : \beta_3 = \beta_4 = 0,$$

and

$$H_A : \beta_3 \neq 0, \text{ or } \beta_4 \neq 0.$$

[2] Pattichis (1999) and Tang and Nair (2002) provide good examples of the use of the bounds test.

Pesaran et al. (2001) establish that the asymptotic distribution of the F-statistic obtained is non-standard under the null hypothesis of no cointegration, regardless of the degree of integration of the variables. They develop two bounds of critical values for the different model specifications (intercept and/or trend): the upper bound applies when all variables are I(1) and the lower bound applies when all variables are I(0). If the computed F-statistic exceeds the upper bound for a chosen significance level, the null hypothesis of no cointegration is rejected. If the F-statistic is inferior to the lower bound, the null hypothesis of no cointegration cannot be rejected. If the F-statistic falls between the two bounds, no conclusive inference can be made and the order of integration of the variables must be determined. The long-run equilibrium is defined as:

$$\beta_3 \mathrm{n} Y_{2t-1} + \beta_4 \ln Y_{1t-1} = 0 . \tag{5.2}$$

5.3 Data

Here we analyze 30 countries from sub-Saharan Africa, 6 countries from Asia, 10 countries from Latin America. The export price index is computed as the ratio of nominal exports (current US Dollars) to real exports (constant US Dollars 1995). The exchange rate is measured as local currency per US Dollar. All data are drawn from the World Development Indicators (World Bank 2003). The sample period extends from 1960 to 2001, though for some countries the period is reduced due to the unavailability of data.

5.4 Empirical Results

5.4.1 Exchange Rate and Export Price

Lag lengths in the unrestricted error correction models are determined through SBIC. Results of the bounds test are displayed in Table 5.1 for the model specification with unrestricted intercept and no trend, and in Table 5.2 for the model specification with unrestricted intercept and unrestricted trend.

Table 5.1. Bounds cointegration test on exchange rate and export price specification: unrestricted intercept and no trend

Country	Lag Length	*F*-Stat
Africa		
Benin	4	0.803
Botswana	1	4.003
Burkina Faso	1	0.837
Burundi	1	1.729
Cameroon	1	4.393
Chad	1	1.542
Comoros	4	3.396
Congo Dem. Rep.	3	10.438***
Congo Rep.	2	0.420
Côte d'Ivoire	1	3.097
Gabon	2	1.053
Gambia	4	4.630
Ghana	1	5.93**
Guinea Bissau	1	2.748
Kenya	1	1.750
Lesotho	1	3.777
Madagascar	2	0.042
Malawi	1	2.283
Mali	2	2.944
Mauritius	1	1.148
Mozambique	1	2.323
Nigeria	1	1.211
Rwanda	1	1.187
Senegal	1	1.272
Sierra Leone	1	2.305
South Africa	2	4.095
Swaziland	1	1.591
Togo	2	3.605
Zambia	4	7.476**
Zimbabwe	2	8.351***
Asia		
Hong Kong	1	1.070
Korea	1	1.622
Philippines	1	3.280
Malaysia	4	0.775
Thailand	4	0.193
Indonesia	3	3.676
Latin America		
Brazil	3	0.932
Mexico	1	1.566
Bolivia	2	6.286**
Colombia	2	0.434

Table 5.1. (cont.)

Country	Lag Length	*F*-Stat
Costa Rica	3	2.722
Paraguay	4	0.699
Uruguay	2	2.218
Dominican Rep.	4	0.980
El Salvador	1	0.213
Venezuela	2	3.681

Notes: Pesaran et al. (2001) provide the critical bounds for the *F*-statistic.
Numbers in parentheses are *p*-values.
***, (**), and [*] indicate significance at 1%, (5%), and [10%].

Table 5.2. Bounds cointegration test on exchange rate and export price specification: unrestricted intercept and unrestricted trend

Country	Lag Length	*F*-Stat
Africa		
Benin	1	2.672
Botswana	1	0.385
Burkina Faso	1	4.496
Burundi	1	6.773*
Cameroon	1	3.632
Chad	1	3.784
Comoros	4	0.996
Congo Dem. Rep.	3	10.823***
Congo Rep.	1	2.941
Côte d'Ivoire	1	2.191
Gabon	1	1.845
Gambia	4	0.492
Ghana	1	6.555*
Guinea Bissau	3	2.404
Kenya	4	7.217
Lesotho	4	6.121
Madagascar	4	4.612
Malawi	1	2.549
Mali	4	1.716
Mauritius	1	2.216
Mozambique	4	5.602
Nigeria	1	2.626
Rwanda	1	0.538
Senegal	1	0.645
Sierra Leone	1	2.322
South Africa	2	1.229
Swaziland	1	2.587

Table 5.2. (cont.)

Country	Lag Length	*F*-Stat
Togo	1	6.088
Zambia	4	4.686
Zimbabwe	1	5.376
Asia		
Hong Kong	1	0.423
Korea	3	3.622
Philippines	1	4.249
Malaysia	1	2.567
Thailand	2	2.977
Indonesia	3	2.379
Latin America		
Brazil	3	2.883
Mexico	1	2.593
Bolivia	2	1.739
Colombia	1	2.874
Costa Rica	3	5.287
Paraguay	4	3.791
Uruguay	3	3.422
Dominican Rep.	1	1.576
El Salvador	1	3.655
Venezuela	4	9.525*

Notes: Pesaran et al. (2001) provide the critical bounds for the *F*-statistic.
***, (**), and [*] indicate significance at 1%, (5%), and [10%].

Table 5.3. Bounds cointegration test on productivity and export price specification: unrestricted intercept and no trend

Country	Lag Length	Bounds Stat
Africa		
Benin	2	0.644
Botswana	2	6.442**
Burkina Faso	1	5.169*
Burundi	3	5.851**
Cameroon	3	1.856
Chad	2	0.054
Congo Dem. Rep.	2	3.072
Congo Rep.	2	0.760
Côte d'Ivoire	2	1.587
Gabon	4	7.861***
Gambia	2	3.840
Ghana	1	5.769*

Table 5.3. (cont.)

Country	Lag Length	Bounds Stat
Guinea Bissau	2	1.249
Kenya	2	0.991
Madagascar	2	0.646
Malawi	2	3.135
Mali	4	6.015**
Mauritius	2	4.444
Mozambique	2	1.100
Nigeria	2	0.995
Rwanda	2	1.723
Senegal	2	2.056
Sierra Leone	2	1.739
South Africa	2	2.349
Swaziland	4	6.176**
Togo	2	7.379**
Zambia	2	3.084
Asia		
Korea	2	2.326
Philippines	2	1.356
Malaysia	2	0.742
Thailand	2	1.487
Indonesia	2	3.609
Latin America		
Brazil	2	5.451*
Mexico	2	1.397
Bolivia	4	7.258**
Colombia	2	1.277
Costa Rica	4	7.311**
Paraguay	2	1.478
Uruguay	2	1.718
Dominican Rep.	2	2.377
Venezuela	2	3.696

Notes: Pesaran et al. (2001) provide the critical bounds for the F-statistic.
***, (**), and [*] indicate significance at 1%, (5%), and [10%].

Table 5.4. Bounds cointegration test on productivity and export price specification: unrestricted intercept and unrestricted trend

Country	Lag Length	Bounds Stat
Africa		
Benin	3	0.680
Botswana	3	2.396

Table 5.4. (cont.)

Country	Lag Length	Bounds Stat
Burkina Faso	3	1.701
Burundi	3	6.011
Cameroon	3	1.218
Chad	4	12.182***
Congo Dem. Rep.	3	11.975***
Congo Rep.	3	2.131
Côte d'Ivoire	3	3.180
Gabon	3	8.196**
Gambia	3	2.724
Ghana	1	6.547*
Guinea Bissau	3	0.206
Kenya	3	2.731
Madagascar	4	9.097**
Malawi	3	1.826
Mali	3	0.681
Mauritius	4	6.648*
Mozambique	4	32.479***
Nigeria	3	2.004
Rwanda	3	1.585
Senegal	3	1.322
Sierra Leone	3	1.431
South Africa	3	4.459
Swaziland	3	3.407
Togo	2	6.972*
Zambia	3	3.002
Asia		
Korea	3	0.016
Philippines	1	6.494*
Malaysia	3	1.633
Thailand	3	3.005
Indonesia	3	1.349
Latin America		
Brazil	3	2.397
Mexico	3	1.408
Bolivia	3	0.988
Colombia	4	9.528**
Costa Rica	4	9.541**
Paraguay	3	1.930
Uruguay	3	2.276
Dominican Rep.	3	2.577
Venezuela	4	8.341**

Notes: Pesaran et al. (2001) provide the critical bounds for the F-statistic.
***, (**), and [*] indicate significance at 1%, (5%), and [10%].

The results are as follows. A cointegration relationship between the exchange rate and export price is found in only 7 out of the 46 countries analyzed.

This cointegrating relation is found in only 5 out of the 30 sub-Saharan African economies studied.

Hence, a devaluation of the local currency does not lead to a lower export price over the long term. The inflationary effects put forward above might offset the drops in export prices denominated in foreign currency by boosting the prices of export products denominated in local currency.

In this case, devaluation is not expected to strengthen trade competitiveness in the long run.

5.4.2 Productivity and Export Price

We then empirically analyze the relationship between productivity and export price. As productivity increase is intrinsically a medium- or long-term process, we apply the "bounds" cointegration test for the empirical investigation. The results are presented in Table 5.3 and Table 5.4. A recapitulation of the results, including the cointegration between the exchange rate and export price, is given in Table 5.5.

The findings can be summarized as follows. A cointegration relationship between productivity and export price is found in 19 out of 41 countries analyzed, while a cointegration between the exchange rate and export price is found in only 7 countries.

Cointegration between productivity and the export price is found in 13 out of the 27 sub-Saharan African economies analyzed, while cointegration between the exchange rate and export price is found in only 5 countries.

Table 5.5. Recapitulation: bounds cointegration test between exchange rate or productivity, and export price

Specification	Exchange Rate and Export Price (Sample: 46 countries)	Productivity and Export Price (Sample: 41 countries)
Constant	5 countries	11 countries
Constant and Trend	4 countries	12 countries
Either of the two specifications	7 countries	19 countries

Note: The table shows number of countries where cointegration is found

5.5 Conclusion

In this chapter, we have analyzed the relationship between exchange rates or productivity and export prices using bounds testing approach developed by Pesaran et al (2001). Empirical results are summarized in Table 5.5. Productivity policy is apparently more effective than devaluation policy in strengthening long-run competitiveness. Domestic inflation may offset the expected effects of the devaluation policy, but productivity improves the fundamentals for long-run international competitiveness.

Having completed our analysis of the first channel of participation in the global economy, international trade, we now turn to the second channel, foreign direct investment (FDI).

References

Engle, R.F. and Granger C.W.J. (1987) Co-integration and error correction: representation, estimation and testing, *Econometrica*, **55**, 251-276.

Johansen, S. and Juselius, K. (1990) Maximum likelihood estimation and inference on cointegration - with applications to the demand for money, *Oxford Bulletin of Economics and Statistics*, **52**, 169-210.

Pattichis, C.A. (1999) Price and income elasticities of disaggregated import demand: results from UECMs and an application, *Applied Economics*, **31**, 1061-1071.

Pesaran M.H., Shin, Y. and Smith, R.J. (2001) Bounds testing approaches to the analysis of level relationships, *Journal of Applied Econometrics*, **16**, 289-326.

Tang, T.C. and Nair, M. (2002) A cointegration analysis of Malaysian import demand function: reassessment from the bounds test, *Applied Economics Letters*, **9**, 293-296.

World Development Indicators, (2003) World Bank, Washington DC.

6 FDI Competitiveness

6.1 Introduction

The inflow of foreign direct investment (FDI) to developing countries has soared over the last decades. From 1990 to 2000 alone, the figure rose from US$24 billion to US$178 billion, or from 24% to 61% of the total foreign investment worldwide. As it turns out, however, the countries of sub-Saharan Africa (SSA) have not received a proportional share. According to UNCTAD (1995), "The African continent did not benefit from the increased investment flows to developing countries as a whole..." Several figures illustrate the magnitude of the disparity: the period averages of FDI inflow into sub-Saharan Africa increased by a mere 59% from 1980–1989 to 1990–1998, while growth rates in developing countries in other parts of the world soared over the same periods (5,200% in the developing countries of Europe and Central Asia, 942% in East Asia and Pacific, 740% in South Asia, 455% in Latin America and the Caribbean, and 672% for the developing world as a whole). Astonishingly, the sub-Saharan African share of total FDI inflow into developing countries plummeted from an average of 36% during 1970–74 to 3% during 1995–99. Table 6.1 traces the changing patters of FDI inflow to developing countries and Africa.

As explained in the theoretical literature, FDI serves as an important engine for growth in developing countries through two main channels: (i) expanding capital stocks in host countries and (ii) bringing employment, managerial skills, and technology.

The first contribution is crucial for countries where incomes and domestic savings are particularly low, such as the countries of sub-Saharan Africa. While these countries vitally depend on external capital for investment and growth, poor credibility and other factors limit their access to the international capital markets. As a consequence, they are forced to rely solely on FDI and official loans as sources of fresh foreign capital. Alarmingly, these sources are now being rapidly depleted. Official loans (as share of GNP) to SSA countries dropped from 6% in 1990 to 3.8% in 1998. Foreign assistance per capita shrunk from US$35 to US$28 from

Table 6.1. Annual averages of net FDI inflow to developing countries, 1970–1999 (millions US$)

FDI inflow	1970–74	1975–79	1980–84
All developing countries	2,058	5,967	8,896
East Asia & Pacific	464	1,034	2,346
Europe & Central Asia	58	65	87
Latin America & Caribbean	1,500	3,496	5,467
South Asia	50	71	163
Sub-Saharan Africa	741	803	866
SSA share (%)	36	13	10
FDI inflow	1985–89	1990–94	1995–99
All developing countries	15,222	25,347	153,805
East Asia & Pacific	5,588	26,352	60,342
Europe & Central Asia	341	4,469	20,784
Latin America & Caribbean	5,960	15,629	59,332
South Asia	350	863	3,693
Sub-Saharan Africa	1,337	1,847	5,170
SSA share (%)	9	4	3

Sources: Asiedu (2002); Global Development Finance, World Bank (2002)

1989–92 to 1993–97. Hence, the need for FDI in the SSA countries now appears to be more urgent than ever before.[1]

Given the importance of FDI inflow for SSA, the countries of the region must find newer and more effective policies to attract foreign investment. Despite its many policy efforts, SSA Africa has received only a small proportion of the global surge of FDI inflow. Measures to strengthen the ability of SSA countries to attract FDI, i.e. "FDI competitiveness," need to be examined. One way to identify effective measures for this purpose is to investigate the factors that determine inflow of FDI into specific regions, countries, or localities.

6.2 Literature Review

Most analyses of the determinants of FDI inflow have included the size of the host markets, measured with GDP. The size of the market has been widely found to be a significant incentive for FDI, and in some cases it has proven to be the most important incentive. A larger market brings in higher returns on investment by allowing a more efficient utilization of resources

[1] Asiedu (2001) and the World Development Report from the World Bank (various issues).

and the exploitation of economies of scale (Moore, 1993; Wang and Swain, 1995; Raggazi, 1973). Chakrabarti (2001) have compiled a relatively comprehensive list of studies which have identified the size of an economy as a considerable determinant of FDI inflow for developed and developing economies alike. The size of the market, however, might be less influential, or even insignificant, when FDI is invested to exploit the host country solely as a production base; that is, to reap profits from the cost advantage of the host economy by exporting the production, more competitively, to markets at home or in third countries (Agarwal, 1980).

A second potential determinant is the movement in the price level. A large and uncontainable increase in the price level, or high inflation, might reflect instability of the macroeconomic policy of the host country. This type of instability creates uncertainty in the investment environment (Bajo-Rubia and Sosvilla-Rivero, 1994; Yang et al., 2000). High inflation discourages FDI for re-exportation since the relative costs of production in the host country rise. In contrast, falling price levels and the resulting contraction in economic activities might trigger a deflationary spiral and eventually bankrupt the host country's firms. This can induce local investors to sell off their interests in the host country's companies to foreign investors at low prices, thereby expanding the inflow of FDI.

A third frequently noted factor is the strength of the host country's currency, measured by exchange rates. A depreciation of the host country currency might attract FDI for two reasons. First, a depreciation of the host country currency renders the shares of host country firms relatively cheap, motivating M&A from foreign firms. Second, in cases where the FDI is invested for re-export to markets at home or in third countries, a depreciation of the host country's currently will enhance the competitiveness of producing in the host country, thereby raising the investors' wealth. In cases where FDI is invested for the sale in the host market, on the other hand, a depreciation of the currency might hinder inflow. Again, there are two reasons for this. First, as FDI is projected over the long-run horizon, the stream of return on investments might fall in terms of the currency of the country of origin. Second, a depreciation of the currency lowers the relative purchasing power of consumers in the host country. All in all, the effects of exchange rate levels on FDI inflow are rather ambiguous (Benassy-Quere et al., 2001).

The volatility of the host country's exchange rates can also be a notable determinant of the extent of incoming FDI. Instability of a currency has often been identified as a significant impediment for the inflow of FDI. Income stream from a highly volatile currency area is associated, in the long run, with high exchange risk (Chakrabarti, 2001). FDI investors lack the security of portfolio investors, as the latter can reduce the risk of exchange rate variability by hedging through the derivative market in the short run. As hedging is impossible in the long run, FDI investors must pay much closer attention to exchange rate volatility. This factor is a particularly robust determinant for risk-averse investors (Benassy-Quere et al., 2001). On the other hand, a policy of maintaining stable nominal exchange rates very often leads to a loss of price competitiveness, leading to another condition which discourages FDI inflow. In the presence of comparatively high inflation, a stable nominal currency hides a cumulated appreciation of the real currency and therefore pushes up real prices. In contrast, a less restrictive policy towards volatility of nominal exchange rates makes it possible to eliminate trends in real exchange rates and maintain price competitiveness. Hence, using the stability of exchange rates as an incentive to attract FDI involves a trade-off between volatility and price competitiveness.

Finally, the instability of the host country currency tends to reduce FDI inflow by discouraging the repatriation of investment returns. On the contrary, a positive relationship between FDI inflow and exchange rate volatility might be found if investment in the local market is used as a substitute to exporting. When variance is judged as too high, one way to escape the vagaries of the currency market is to produce through FDI into the local market. In the short run, larger volatility will lead to greater FDI inflow. In the long run, however, the negative effects of volatility in attracting FDI will outweigh the positive effects due to the mechanisms described above (Harvey, 1990).

A straightforward incentive for foreign investors is the level of capital return in the host country. FDI will flow into a country that can offer a higher rate of return. However, measuring the rate of capital return can be a daunting task in developing countries, especially in Africa, a region lacking effective capital markets. One way to overcome the challenge is to employ the inverse of GDP as a proxy. Asiedu (2002) explains the reasoning behind this approach. When the capital return is assumed to be equal to the marginal product of capital, a country with scarcer capital will turn out to have proportionally higher return. Given that a lower income level induces smaller capital stock, investment in low-income countries can be expected to yield high return. This, in turn, justifies the use of the inverse of GDP as a proxy for capital return. The observed facts support this reasoning. According to UNCTAD (1995), FDI from the USA in 1990 to 1993 gained considerably higher average returns in the developing world (17%) than in the developed world (10%). Table 6.2 presents the different rates of return on capital in various regions in more detail. Taken as a whole, the data support the argument that lower income countries produce higher capital returns.

Table 6.2. Rates of return on US FDI, 1991–96

Region	1991	1992	1993
Africa	30.6	28.4	25.8
Asia & Pacific	23.8	22.6	20.7
Latin America & Caribbean	12.2	14.3	14.9
Developing Countries	15.9	17.2	16.9
All countries	11.6	10.4	11.1
Region	1994	1995	1996
Africa	24.6	35.3	34.2
Asia & Pacific	18.4	20.2	19.3
Latin America & Caribbean	15.3	13.1	12.8
Developing Countries	16.5	15.8	15.3
All countries	11.7	13.3	12.5

Source: UNCTAD (1999)

6.3 Empirical Analysis

In this section we present an empirical analysis of the FDI determinants in sub Saharan African (SSA) economies and selected economies of Asia and Latin America. Referring to the list of variables raised in the literature review and the explicit relationship shown in the theoretical model of Lucas (1993), we introduce the following variables as potential determinants of FDI in our analysis: total factor productivity (TFP) measured with the Solow residuals, exchange rate (EXC) measured with the host country's currency per US Dollar, inflation measured with the consumer price index (CPI), volatility of CPI (VolCPI) measured with the variance, trade share (TRS) measured with the ratio of the sum of exports and imports over GDP, capital return or rental measured with the inverse of GDP, and the market size measured with GDP. The selection of variables was dictated in part by the availability of data. We use annual data covering 1980 to 2001. We use the data of the following 41 countries: Benin; Botswana; Burkina Faso; Burundi; Cameroon; Chad; Democratic Republic of the Congo; Republic of the Congo; Cote d'Ivoire; Gabon; Gambia; Ghana; Guine Bisau; Kenya; Madagascar; Malawi; Mali; Mauritius; Mozambique; Nigeria; Rwanda; Senegal; Siera Leone; South Africa; Swaziland; Togo; Zambia; Korea; Philipines; Malaysia; Thailand; Indonesia; Brazil; Mexico; Bolivia; Colombia; Costa Rica; Paraguay; Uruguay; Dominican Republic; Venezuela.

We employ the panel cointegration test suggested by Pedroni (2001). The technique starts by estimating the following equation using ordinary least squares:[2]

$$\begin{aligned} FDI = \beta_0 + \beta_1 TFP + \beta_2 EXC + \beta_3 CPI + \beta_4 VolCPI \\ + \beta_5 TRS + \beta_6 (1/GDP) + \beta_7 [(1/GDP) \times D_1] \\ + \beta_8 [(1/GDP) \times D_2] + u_t, \end{aligned} \tag{6.1}$$

where D_1 and D_2 are dummy variables, respectively, for Asia and Africa, and u_t is the error term.

Then, the residuals from the regression equation are collected to construct a new panel data. The panel unit root test proposed by Levin et al. (2002) is carried out on the newly constructed panel data. A rejection of the null hypothesis of unit root would indicate that the variables in (6.1) are cointegrated and that estimated relationship represents an equilibrium long-term relationship. The technique depicts and focuses on a unique cointegration equation although there might exist multiple cointegrating equations.

The results of the empirical investigation are displayed in Table 6.3. Three specifications are examined: the first is a specification without distinction between the countries in the analysis; the second, a specification with a dummy variable for the Asian countries; and the third, a specification with distinct dummy variables for respectively Asian and African countries. The dummy variables are applied to the coefficient on the inverse of GDP, to make the latter reflect either capital return or market size. We also attempted to apply the dummy variables on the intercept as well as on the other slope coefficients, but no distinguished features appeared.

The results of the panel cointegration test are given under the Levin and Lin statistic displayed at the bottom of each specification. The null hypothesis of the existence of a unit root in the residuals is rejected for all three specifications. Hence, we can conclude that the variables are cointegrated. The estimated equations, particularly the third specification, represent the long-run equilibrium relationship between FDI inflow and the related potential determinants. This specification allows us to make the following assessments.

---

[2] More formal explanation of panel cointegration tests will be given in Chaps. 8, 9 and 10.

Table 6.3. Determinants FDI, panel cointegration test

	Spec 1	Spec 2	Spec 3
Constant	19.761***	22.273***	21.31***
	(10.087)	(10.791)	(10.276)
TFP	0.792***	0.799***	0.777**
	(2.394)	(2.434)	(2.381)
Exchange Rate	0.0001***	0.00006***	0.00006***
	(3.288)	(3.584)	(3.82)
CPI	–0.00002*	–0.00002*	–0.00002*
	(–1.607)	(–1.776)	(–1.813)
Volatility of CPI	–0.022***	–0.022***	–0.024***
	(–8.085)	(–8.116)	(–8.707)
Trade Share	0.003*	0.001	0.001
	(0.061)	(0.713)	(0.357)
1/GDP	0.539***	0.735***	0.154
	(6.232)	(7.244)	(0.745)
$D_1(1/GDP)$ - Asia		–0.617***	–0.057
		(–3.621)	–0.235
$D_2(1/GDP)$ - Africa			0.759***
			(3.221)
Adjusted R^2	0.935	0.936	0.936
F-stat	249.153	248.102	246.256
Levin and Lin Stat	–8.876	–8.268	–8.326
	[0.001]	[0.001]	[0.001]

Notes: Numbers in ( ) and [ ] are t-statistic and p-value, respectively.
***(**)[*] indicate significance level at 1% (5%) [10%].

Both the total factor productivity (TFP) and exchange rate, the main focuses of our analysis, appear as strong determinants of inflow of foreign investment. An increase in TFP pulls down the productivity-adjusted wage, as well as several other variables. As shown in various theoretical models, this decrease in wage opens up incentives for the inflow of foreign investment. Enhanced productivity diminishes the per-unit cost of production and allows larger profit margins for investments. Results with respect to the exchange rate imply that a depreciation of the local currency invites an inflow of FDI. Currency depreciation permits foreign investments to acquire locally existing firms and to establish new Greenfield plants at lower prices in foreign currency. Depreciation also reduces the cost of production in the host country relative to the cost in other locations. The incentives from exchange rate depreciation are particularly important for firms which use the host country as a production base and export the products to markets at home (origin) or in third countries.

Our results suggest that both productivity policy and exchange rate policy can be effective in sharpening FDI competitiveness, *i.e.* in attracting foreign investments. The level and volatility of CPI can both discourage inflow of FDI. From the viewpoint of foreign investors, high inflation and high CPI volatility are likely to be perceived as signs of unstable domestic macroeconomic conditions. Trade share weakly determines FDI inflow.

An important finding emerges from the inverse of GDP and the dummy variables. The coefficient on the variable is positive and highly significant for the sub-Saharan African economies. This is a strong indication that the capital return plays a far more important role than the market size in attracting foreign investment into Africa. Indeed, by the reasoning explicated above, the countries with the lowest GDPs in the present sample, that is, the countries of sub-Saharan Africa, can be expected to have the thinnest stock of capital and the smallest capital-labor ratio, hence the highest rate of return on capital. This stands to reason, as a high return on capital is one of the consequential incentives for FDI. In this scenario, foreign investments use the SSA countries as a production base and export their products rather than targeting the SSA market itself (the level of GDP). In contrast, the sign of the variable (inverse of GDP) is negative for the Asian countries, suggesting that GDP itself (as opposed to its inverse) appears as a determinant of FDI inflow. The market size seems to be the main incentive for FDI inflow in the presently studied Asia economies; indeed, these countries exhibit the highest GDP in our sample.

The results of our analysis of trade competitiveness have shown that productivity policy is more effective than exchange rate policy, chiefly because the latter may generate inflation which can potentially offset its beneficial effects. In our analysis of FDI competitiveness, on the other hand, both policies have been found to be significant determinants of FDI inflow, *i.e.* both policies can be employed to enhance the ability of the country to attract foreign investment.[3]

6.4 Conclusion

Given the low level of domestic savings and the decreasing per-capita foreign aid in sub-Saharan Africa, FDI in the region is expected not only to provide numerous benefits for the recipient economies, but to play a

[3] More detailed research will have to be conducted to investigate the differences among the magnitudes of contributions of the respective policies.

crucial role in bringing in fresh foreign capital. Discouragingly, however, only a tiny fraction of the recent surge in worldwide foreign investment over the past decades has flown into the SSA countries. The facts at hand implicate the weak competitiveness of SSA countries in attracting FDI. This chapter has pointed out a number of measures which may help to strengthen this competitiveness in the region. Most notably, our findings underline the importance of policy measures to enhance total factor productivity. Another approach is to implement the exchange rate policy. Macroeconomic stability and an open trade policy can be expected to positively affect FDI inflow.

Lastly, we demonstrate that the relatively high rate of return on investment in SSA countries can provide incentive for FDI. This incentive needs to be realized and complemented through the policy measures of the type described above.[4]

References

Agarwal, J.P. (1980) Determinants of foreign direct investment: A survey, *Weltwirtschaftliches Archiv*, **116**, 739-773.

Asiedu, E. (2002) On the development of foreign investment to developing countries: Is Africa different, *World Development*, **30**, 107-119.

Bajo-Rubia, O. and Sosvilla-Rivero, S. (1994) An economic analysis of foreign direct investment in Spain, *Southern Economic Journal*, **61**, 104-117.

Benassy-Quere, A., Fontagne, L. and Lahreche-Revil, A. (2001) Exchange rate strategies in the competition for attracting foreign direct investment, *Journal of the Japanese and International Economics*, **15**, 178-198.

Chakrabarti, A. (2001) The determinants of foreign direct investment: sensitivity analyses of cross-country regressions, *Kyklos*, **54**, 89-114.

Global Development Finance, (2002) World Bank, Washington DC.

Harvey, J.T. (1990) The determinants of direct foreign investment, *Journal of Post Keynesian Economics*, **12**, 260-272.

Levin, A., Chien-Fu, L. and Chia-Shang, J.C. (2002) Unit root tests in panel data: Asymptotic and finite-sample properties, *Journal of Econometrics*, **108**, 1-24.

Lucas, R.E.B. (1993) On the determinations of direct foreign investment: Evidence from East and Southern Asia, *World Development*, **21**, 391-406.

Moore, M.O. (1993) Determinants of German manufacturing direct investment: 1980-1988, *Weltwirtschaftliches Archiv*, **129**, 120-137.

Pedroni, P. (2001) Purchasing power parity tests in cointegrated panels, *Review of Economics and Statistics*, **83**, 727-731.

[4] This chapter is a substantially revised version of Razafimahefa and Hamori (2005).

Razafimahefa, I. F. and Hamori, S. (2005) An empirical analysis of FDI competitiveness in Sub–Saharan Africa and developing countries, *Economics Bulletin*, **6**, 1-8.
Ragazzi, G. (1973) Theories of the determinants of foreign direct investment, *IMF Staff Papers*, **20**, 471-498.
UNCTA (1995) *World Investment Report 1995: Transnational Corporations and Competitiveness / With Overview*, United Nations, New York.
Wang, Z.Q. and Swain, N.J. (1995) The determinants of foreign direct investment in transforming economies: Empirical evidence from Hungary and China, *Weltwirtschaftliches Archiv*, **131**, 359-82.
World Development Report, (various issues), World Bank, Washington DC.
Yang, J.Y.Y., Groenewold, N. and Tcha, M. (2000) The determinants of foreign direct investment in Australia, *Economic Record*, **76**, 45-54.

7 Productivity Determinants

7.1 Introduction

In this chapter, we analyze the channels through which policy makers can directly act to enhance aggregate productivity. Specifically, we consider the following variables as channels to enhance total factor productivity: human capital, reallocation of production factors, agglomeration economies, demographic age structure, infrastructure development, and black market premium in the exchange rate market.

7.2 Literature Review

We investigate six major determinants of productivity. Some are often cited in the literature; others are rather new.

The first is human capital stock. Three models can be used to clarify the effects of human capital on productivity (Wolff, 2000): the human capital model, catch-up model, and interaction-with-technical-change model.

Second is the reallocation of production factors. Such reallocation has frequently been considered in growth theory (e.g. see Chenery, Robinson, and Syrquin, 1986). Young (1995) showed that inter-sectoral reallocations of one production factor, labor, drove a large part of TFP growth in East Asia from the 1960s to the early 1990s. Poirson (1998) found a high correlation between growth and the reallocation of the labor force from agricultural to non-agricultural activities.

Third is agglomeration economies. This determinant of productivity can be classified into three groups: (i) at the firm level from improved access to market centers, (ii) at the industry level from intra-industry localization economies, and (iii) at the regional level from inter-industry urbanization economies (Lall et al., 2004). The locations and geographic concentrations of economic activity have attracted strong interest in recent years. The analyses are essentially based on regional and location theory (Krugman, 1991; Fujita et al., 1999; Weber, 1909; Hotelling, 1929; Greenhut and Greenhut, 1975; Isard, 1956). Increasing return to scale is viewed as the main channel towards the spatial concentration of economic activities and enhanced productivity. (Fujita and Thisse, 1996).

Fourth is the demographic age structure. Kogel (2005) found that total factor productivity rises when the growth rate of the total population shifts from higher to lower relative to the growth rate of the working population. The East Asia countries experienced this phenomenon after World War II (Bloom and Williamson, 1998). The growth rates of the total populations in those countries exceeded the growth rates of the working age populations until the mid-1960s. Thereafter, from about the mid-1970s, the tendency was reversed. This demographic change has been described as a significant contributor to the productivity and economic growth of East Asia. Two channels can be put forward. First, a rising ratio of the working age population to the total population increases the ratio of "producers" to "consumers" and contributes positively to growth of output per capita. Second, the demographic change allows each producer to save a larger share of its production output, which in turn increases the capital per labor ratio and increases productivity.

Fifth is infrastructure development. Infrastructure is frequently pointed out in the literature as a crucial factor underlying total factor productivity. Extended infrastructure reduces the direct and indirect costs of production. Infrastructure is included among the seven factors identified as "drivers of industrial competitiveness" (UNIDO, 2002). The availability of infrastructure is a precondition for the development of the industrial sector in any country. As explained in the Global Competitiveness Report (GCR, 2003), expansion of industries requires two main favorable environments: a microeconomic or business environment including regulations, and a macroeconomic environment including infrastructure. Hazell and Fan (2002) stress the importance of developing infrastructure for agricultural activities to counterbalance the frequent bias of infrastructure development towards industrialization.

The sixth determinant of productivity is the black market premium in the exchange rate market, which reflects the degree of distortions in domestic prices. Market distortions can be expected to impede efficient allocations of resources and thereby hamper productivity. Governments in developing countries often alter price structures to create favorable conditions for specific sectors in their economies or specific groups in their societies. The patterns of relative prices are also sometimes modified to promote the import substitution sector. Under an export-based policy, governments influence price structures by implementing measures to create incentives for the export sector. When governments rush to open their sectors to international markets, relative prices are often biased voluntarily in favor of tradable goods and at the expense of non-tradable goods. Also, due to political motives or policy objectives, governments frequently lower the prices of rural agricultural goods relative to urban industrial goods in order to secure support from politically strong urban populations. However, it is also important to note that a change in relative prices in the opposite direction would also be harmful. A naturally arising relative price can be expected to bring about the optimal allocation of resources.[1]

7.3 Data

Here we analyze how TFP growth relates to the seven determinants of productivity described above in 27 economies in sub-Saharan Africa. These are Benin; Botswana; Burkina Faso; Burundi; Cameroon; Chad; Democratic Republic of the Congo; Republic of the Congo; Côte d'Ivoire; Gabon; Gambia; Ghana; Guinee Bissau; Kenya; Madagascar; Malawi; Mali; Mauritius; Mozambique; Nigeria; Rwanda; Senegal; South Africa; Swaziland; Togo; Zambia; Zimbabwe.

Lacking similar data for comparison, we exclude the Asian and Latin American economies from this analysis. The sample constitutes annual data spanning the period from 1965 to 1999. TFP is measured by the Solow residuals. The variables used as proxies for the TFP determinants are taken from the World Bank Africa Database (2001). The following methods were used to measure each variable.

Human capital is measured based on the illiteracy rate among the population aged 15 years old or over. Questions on the functional utility of "merely" literate workers might give rise to controversy on the effectiveness of illiteracy reduction in influencing productivity. Though the level of secondary or higher education may be preferable as a measure of human capital, data of this type are unavailable for the entire period sampled. Thus, we have no choice but to rely on the illiteracy rate. In any case, an increase in secondary or higher schooling reflects a higher government priority on education, a factor likely to be strongly correlated with illiteracy.

---

[1] Economic diversification may be another determinant of productivity. This is defined as the spreading of production to a growing number of different outputs that do not necessarily imply different productivity levels. As the standard models from Romer (1990) show, diversification can be treated as a production factor in itself as an enhancer of productivity for both labor and human capital. Romer constructs a model of economy with three sectors: a final goods sector, an intermediate goods sector, and a research sector. The research sector develops and provides advanced technologies for the intermediate goods sector, thereby increasing the variety of intermediate goods produced. This diversification in intermediate goods enhances the productivity of the final good sector.

Reallocation of production is based on the share of the manufacturing value-added in the total GDP. Straightforward measures of capital and labor use in each of the sectors would give more accurate insight. Again, however, these data are unavailable. Given that the share of production factors employed in each sector determines the share in total production, the share of manufacturing value-added in the total GDP is arguably an accurate reflection of the pattern of reallocation.

Agglomeration economies are proxied with the share of the urban population in the total population. A direct measure of industry agglomeration, such as the number of existing clusters or industry densities (the numbers of industries in specific areas), would be preferable. Again, however, the data are unavailable from the countries in our sample. By adapting the reasoning of Krugman (1991), Fujita et al. (1999) and Lall et al. (2004), we assume that industries concentrate in locations which permit easy access to, and low transport cost for, inputs such as labor. A higher concentration of labor, such as an increase in the share of urban population, is thus likely to increase the concentration of industries in a given area.

The demographic age structure is measured by the age dependency ratio, i.e. the ratio of dependents (under 15 and over 60) to the working age population (between 15 and 60).

The level of infrastructure development is captured by the number of main telephone lines per thousand people. The available data on other potentially useful measures, such as kilometers of paved roads or electricity supply, do not cover the entire sample period.

The black market premium is measured by the ratio of the parallel exchange rate to the official exchange rate.

7.4 Empirical Analysis

We employ the panel Granger causality test suggested by Hurlin and Venet (2001) to examine the relationship between the TFP growth in SSA economies and the potential determinants.

The panel unit root test is carried out for each of the variables before the causality test, in accordance with the method of Levin et al. (2002).[2] Table 7.1 presents the results of the panel unit root tests. The following variables are found to be stationary in level form: TFP growth, the share of manufacturing value-added in the total GDP, the ratio of the parallel exchange rate to the official exchange rate, the age dependency ratio, the illiteracy

[2] More formal explanation of panel unit root tests will be given in Chaps. 8, 9 and 10.

rate, and the ratio of urban to total population. The number of phone lines per thousand people is found to include one unit root. Hence, all of the variables are introduced in the causality test in level form,[3] with the exception of the infrastructure variable used in first difference.

Table 7.2 presents the results of the test on the causality from the potential determinants to TFP growth.

First, we find that enhancements in manufacturing industries influence aggregate productivity. Reallocation of production factors leads to the restructuring of an economy and pulls up productivity through two channels: the direct channel, the intrinsically higher productivity of the manufacturing sector compared to the agriculture and service sectors; and the indirect channel, the spreading externality effects of the manufacturing sector on the productivity of other sectors in the economy.

Table 7.1. Productivity determinants, unit root test (Levin, Lin and Chu Test)

Variables	Constant & Trend	Constant	None
TFP growth	–18.378***	–25.241***	–47.563***
Manuf. Value Added	–0.650	–2.492***	–0.358
Black Market Premium	–97.056***	–67.29***	–0.850
Age Dependency Ratio	–0.527	–1.135	–1.955**
Illiteracy Rate	3.660	10.103	–9.207***
Urban Pop. Ratio	–5.476***	–2.304***	1.910
Phone Line	9.324	18.015	13.405
Phone Line (first difference)	–3.864***	–0.786	–3.007***

Note: ***(**) indicates significance at the 1% (5%) level

Table 7.2. Productivity determinants, causality test (dependent variable: TFP growth)

Excluded Variables	*F* statistic	*p*-value
Manuf. Value Added	3.305	0.011
Black Market Premium	2.578	0.037
Age Dependency Ratio	0.386	0.819
Illiteracy Rate	0.441	0.779
Urban Pop. Ratio	8.326	0.001
Phone Line	8.942	0.001

[3] Given that the age dependency ratio and the illiteracy rate are only stationary in level form under the "none" specification, we also verified the causality test using the first difference form of those two variables. The thrust of the results has not been altered.

Second, the black market premium measured by the ratio of the parallel exchange rate to the official exchange rate impacts aggregate productivity. Distortions arising from factors underlying larger black market premiums impede the optimal allocation of resources and hinder productivity growth.

Third, agglomeration economies measured by the ratios of urban to total populations affect TFP growth. The concentration of production factors (here measured with labor) stimulates the concentration of industries, which in turn creates and widens the scope for productivity growth. Firms and workers both benefit when the former locate themselves in areas with concentrated labor. Lower transport cost is just one of the benefits. A higher concentration of labor give firms a wider choice of workers, and the firms drawn into an area to take advantage of the labor pool give the workers a wider choice of employers. The overall scenario improves both efficiency and productivity in an entire area, and the formation of similar agglomerations in various parts of a country benefits an economy as a whole. Policies to promote the concentration of production factors and industries are highly recommendable for the SSA countries. These policies can include the creation of industrial zones through the development of specific infrastructures, or the creation of tax free zones using specific tax treatments.

Fourth, we find the causality relationship from the availability of infrastructure to aggregate productivity. It is important to note that the sole availability of infrastructure might not accurately reflect the need for higher productivity. The functionality of the existing infrastructure is more important.

Finally, we find no causal relationships from the age-dependency ratio and illiteracy rate to aggregate productivity. We plan to investigate these relationships further in future research.

We also analyze the reverse causal relationship from TFP growth to each of the factors mentioned above. Table 7.3 presents the results. With the exception of the infrastructure variable, no reverse causal relationship is depicted. These results support our assessment that factors raised here can indeed serve as primary policy tools to enhance the aggregate productivity of an economy.

Table 7.3. Productivity determinants, reverse causality (excluded variable: TFP growth)

Dependent Variables	*F* statistic	*p*-value
Manuf. Value added	1.218	0.302
Black Market Premium	1.054	0.379
Age Dependency Ratio	0.621	0.648
Illiteracy Rate	0.651	0.626
Urban Pop. Ratio	1.263	0.283
Phone Line	2.201	0.068

7.5 Conclusion

In this chapter, we sought direct policy measures to increase productivity by investigating the determinants of productivity. Besides the usual factors such as human capital, infrastructure, and price distortions, we delved into three other factors which have yet to be sufficiently considered in the literature: agglomeration economies, reallocation of production factors, and demographic age structure.

Human capital is measured based on the illiteracy rate among the population aged 15 years old or over. Reallocation of production is based on the share of the manufacturing value-added in the total GDP. Agglomeration economies are proxied with the share of the urban population in the total population. The demographic age structure is measured by the age dependency ratio, i.e. the ratio of dependents (under 15 and over 60) to the working age population (between 15 and 60). The level of infrastructure development is captured by the number of main telephone lines per thousand people. The black market premium is measured by the ratio of the parallel exchange rate to the official exchange rate.

Empirical results show that reallocation of production, black market premium, agglomeration economies, and the level of infrastructure development are significant factors to increase productivity.

References

Bloom, D.E. and Williamson, J.G. (1998) Demographic transitions and economic miracles in emerging Asia, *World Bank Economic Review*, **12**, 419-56.

Chenery, H., Robinson, S. and Syrquin, M. (1986) *Industrialization and Growth: A Comparative Study*, Oxford University Press, London.

Fujita, M., Krugman, P. and Venables, A.J. (1999) *The Spatial Economy: Cities, Regions and International Trade*, MIT Press, Cambridge, MA.

Fujita, M. and Thisse, J.F. (1996) Economics of agglomeration, *Journal of the Japanese and International Economies*, **10**, 339-78.

Global Competitiveness Report (2003) World Economic Forum.

Greenhut, J. and Greenhut, M.L. (1975) Spatial price discrimination, competition and locational effects, *Economica*, **42**, 401-419.

Hazell, P.B.R. and Fan, S. (2002) The importance of public investments and institutions for the functioning of food markets in developing countries, In Lutz, Clemens, ed. *Food Markets and Food Security in West Africa,* CDS Research Report 15, 99-115. Centre for Development Studies (CSD).

Hotelling, H. (1929) Stability in competition, *Economic Journal*, **39**, 41-57.

Hurlin, C. and Venet, B. (2001) Granger causality test in Panel data models with fixed coefficients, Miméo, University Paris IX.

Isard, W. (1956) *Location and Space-Economy*, MIT Press, Cambridge, MA.
Kogel, T. (2005) Youth dependency and total factor productivity, *Journal of Development Economics*, **76**, 147-173.
Krugman, P. (1991) Increasing returns and economic geography, *Journal of Political Economy*, **99**, 483-99.
Lall, S.V., Shalizi, Z. and Deichmann, U. (2004) Agglomeration economies and productivity in Indian industry, *Journal of Development Economics*, **73**, 643-73.
Levin, A., Lin, F. and Chu, C. (2002) Unit root tests in Panel data: Asymptotic and finite sample properties, *Journal of Econometrics*, **108**, 1-24.
Poirson, H. (1998) Essais en Economie de la Croissance et du développement, PhD Thesis, EHESS, Paris.
Romer, P. (1990) Endogenous technological change, *Journal of Political Economy*, **98**, 71-102.
UNIDO (2002) *Industrial Development Report*, United Nations Industrial Development Organization, Austria.
Weber, M. (1909) *The Agrarian Sociology of Ancient Civilizations*, translated by R.I. Frank, (Verso, London).
Wolff, E.N. (2000) Human capital investment and economic growth: Exploring the cross-country evidence, *Structural Change and Economic Dynamics*, **11**, 433-72.
World Bank Africa Database (2001) World Bank, Washington DC.
Young, A. (1995) The tyranny of numbers: Confronting the statistical realities of the east Asian growth experience, *Quarterly Journal of Economics*, **110**, 641-80.

8 Sustainability of Trade Accounts

8.1 Introduction

Trade deficits pose difficulties not only for developing countries, but also for industrialized countries such as the U.S. and the countries of Europe. As economies grow, their demand for foreign goods grows in parallel and world trade benefits as a whole. Any problems which appear derive not from rising imports, but from the mismatch between export and import growth. Without a stable balance between exports and imports, a newly emerging trade deficit will tend to expand.

We use the concept of cointegration to examine changes in the trade accounts of sub-Saharan African countries. Specifically, we seek to determine whether changes in the trade accounts of sub-Saharan Africa are temporary or permanent. If the changes in the trade accounts are temporary, then exports and imports are cointegrated and the changes are self-correcting. If the changes in trade accounts are permanent, then exports and imports are not cointegrated and the changes are explosive.

This type of analysis is important from a policy perspective, but only when the changes in trade accounts are permanent. When changes in trade accounts are temporary, the imbalances in the trade account converge toward equilibrium over the long run. When the changes are permanent, however, the trade deficits gradually expand. In the former case, short-run trade deficits do not pose significant policy problems. In the latter, governments must use macroeconomic policies to control the changes in trade accounts.

Several groups have analyzed the problem of negative trade accounts. Mann (2002), for example, has published an excellent survey on the topic. Only a few papers, however, have addressed the idea of long-run equilibrium between exports and imports. The study by Husted (1992) is probably the most important among those so far published. In an analysis of quarterly U.S. data from 1967 to 1989 using the Engle and Granger test (Engle and Granger, 1987), Husted (1992) identified a long-run equilibrium between exports and imports. This result shows that U.S. trade deficits are temporary and that the imbalances of the U.S. trade account converge toward equilibrium over the long run. It also indicates that trade deficits are sustainable as a whole. Even without macroeconomic policies to correct deficits in the U.S. trade account, equilibrium seems to be achieved in the long run.

Arize (2002) investigated the long-run convergence between imports and exports in 50 countries (including nine African countries) over the quarterly period between 1973 and 1998.[1] This study finds evidence of cointegration between imports and exports for the majority of the countries, and supports the view of Husted (1992). This indicates that these countries are not in violation of their international budget constraint. The evidence further suggests that imports and exports are cointegrated, not just in low income countries but in middle-income and high-income countries as well. Empirical results concerning constancy of the cointegrating space are robust to income classification.

Irandoust and Ericsson (2004) also expanded on Husted's (1992) analysis by focusing on a larger sample set of six countries—the U.S., Germany, the U.K., France, Sweden, and Italy—between 1971 and 1997. Their objective was to search for cointegrating relationships between exports and imports in those countries using the Johansen and Juselius test (Johansen, 1988; Johansen and Juselius, 1990). Cointegrating relationships between exports and imports were found in Germany, the U.S., and Sweden. This implies that these countries are not in violation of their international budget constraint and that trade imbalances are short-run phenomena and, in the long-run, are sustainable.

In this chapter we empirically analyze trade account issues in the countries of sub-Saharan Africa. In doing so, we are forced to rely extensively on analyses with the panel unit root test.[2] Standard unit root tests lack robustness with small samples, and limitations of available data from sub-Saharan Africa pose serious challenges for analyses of the region (often only annual data can be used). By applying the panel unit root test, however, we can perform both time series and cross section analyses without limiting the power of our analyses due to a small sample size.

---

[1] These nine African countries are Burundi, Ethiopia, Kenya, Mauritius, Morocco, Nigeria, South Africa, Tunisia, and Zambia.

[2] Phillips and Moon (2000) and Baltagi (2005, Chap. 12) are good reference for nonstationary panel data analysis.

8.2 Basic Model

Following Husted (1992), Arize (2002), and Irandoust and Ericsson (2004), we examine the international budget constraint for analyzing the dynamics of the trade balance. These studies show that the international budget constraint for a given country can be written as follow:

$$EX_t = \beta_0 + \beta_1 IM_t + u_t, \tag{8.1}$$

where EX_t is exports at time t, IM_t is imports at time t, and u_t is the disturbance at time t. Under the null hypothesis states that the economy satisfies its international budget constraint, it is expected that $\beta_1 = 1$ and u_t is a stationary process. In other words, if exports and imports are non-stationary variables, then under the null hypothesis they are cointegrated with a cointegrating vector (1,-1).

8.3 Data

This chapter analyzes 30 sub-Saharan African countries, i.e. Benin; Botswana; Burkina Faso; Burundi; Cameroon; Cape Verde; Central African Rep.; Chad; Republic of the Congo; Côte d'Ivoire; Equatorial Guinea; Gabon; Gambia; Kenya; Madagascar; Malawi; Mali; Mauritius; Niger; Nigeria; Rwanda; Senegal; Seychelles; Sierra Leone; South Africa; Swaziland; Tanzania; Togo; Zambia; Zimbabwe. We use annual data from between 1960 and 2004. The data were obtained from the International Financial Statistics (CD ROM; International Monetary Foundation). Exports and imports are both expressed in terms of US $ millions. Table 8.1 shows the countries and their sample periods.

Figures 8.1 through 8.30 show the trade balance movements in each country. Trade deficits are clearly a problem for many of the countries of sub-Saharan Africa, and in many cases the deficits levels start to climb from around the 1980's. Taking this into account, we divide the study period into three sample periods for the empirical analysis:

[Sample A]: 1960–2004,
[Sample B]: 1960–1980,
[Sample C]: 1981–2004.

Sample A is the total sample period. Sample B and Sample C correspond to the first half and second half, respectively.

Table 8.1. Country and sample period

Country	Sample Period
Benin	1960–2004
Botswana	1960–1998
Burkina Faso	1960–2003
Burundi	1960–2004
Cameroon	1960–2002
Cape Verde	1960–2001
Central African Rep.	1960–2002
Chad	1960–2002
Congo Rep.	1960–2000
Côte d'Ivoire	1960–2003
Equatorial Guinea	1960–2000
Gabon	1960–2001
Gambia	1960–2002
Kenya	1960–2003
Madagascar	1960–2003
Malawi	1964–2003
Mali	1960–2003
Mauritius	1960–2004
Niger	1960–2003
Nigeria	1960–2004
Rwanda	1960–2004
Senegal	1960–2003
Seychelles	1960–2003
Sierra Leone	1960–2004
South Africa	1960–2003
Swaziland	1965–2002
Tanzania	1960–2004
Togo	1960–2004
Zambia	1960–2000
Zimbabwe	1964–2001

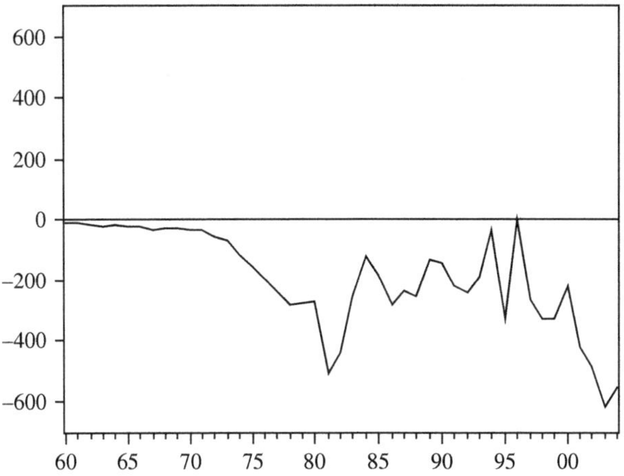

Fig. 8.1. Trade balance (US millions): Benin

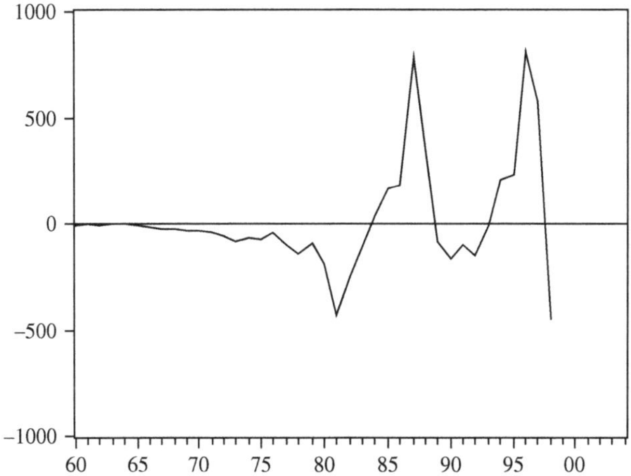

Fig. 8.2. Trade balance (US millions): Botswana

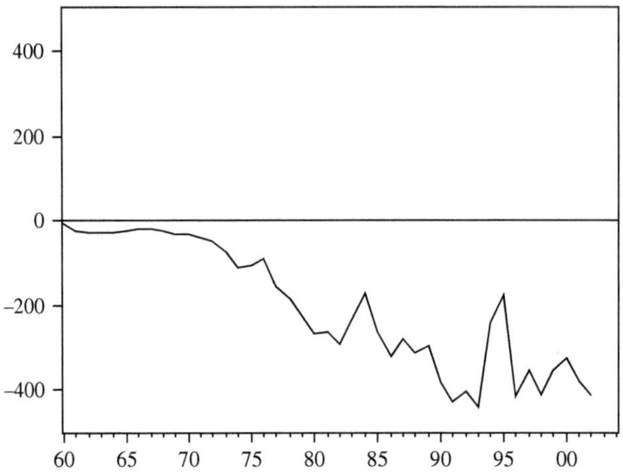

Fig. 8.3. Trade balance (US millions): Burkina Faso

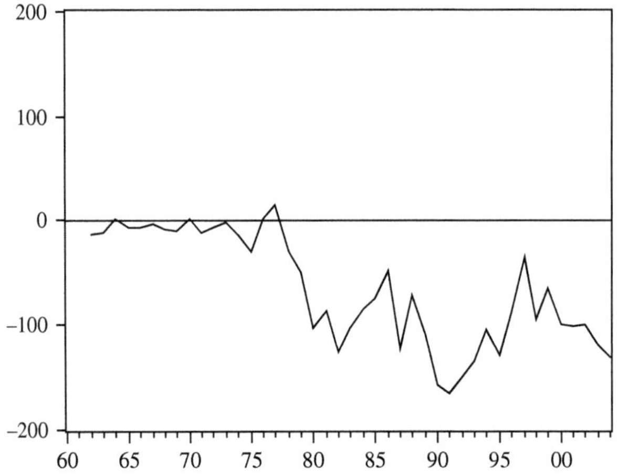

Fig. 8.4. Trade balance (US millions): Burundi

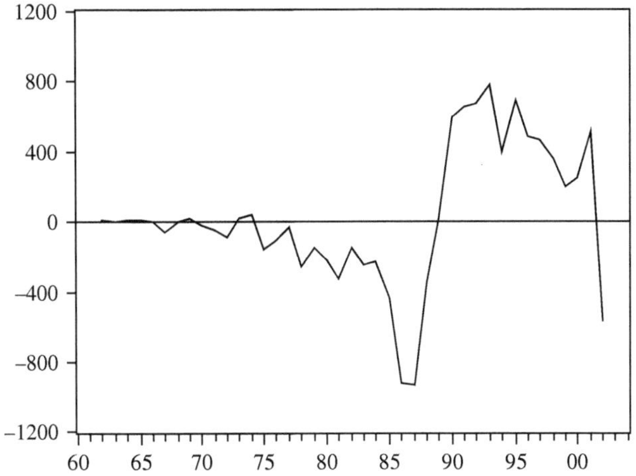

Fig. 8.5. Trade balance (US millions): Cameroon

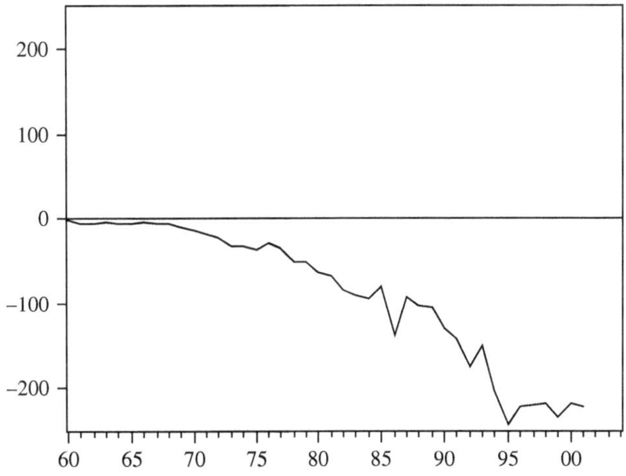

Fig. 8.6. Trade balance (US millions): Cape Verde

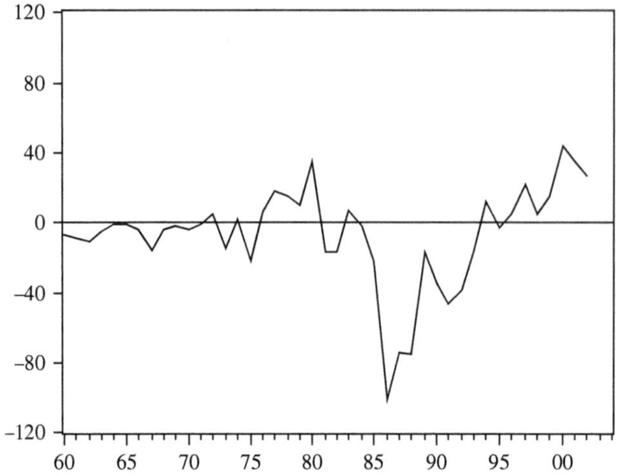

Fig. 8.7. Trade balance (US millions): Central African Rep.

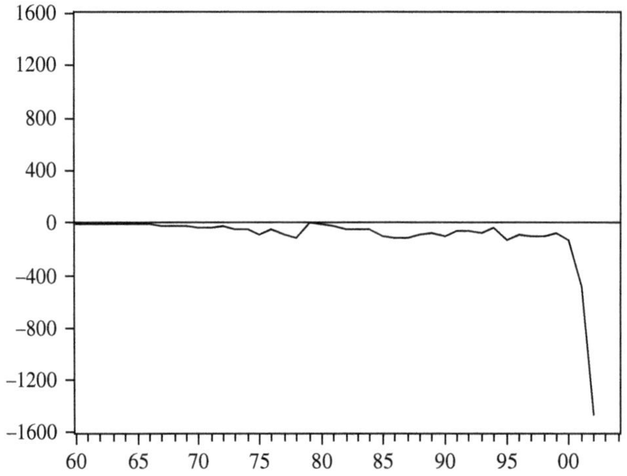

Fig. 8.8. Trade balance (US millions): Chad

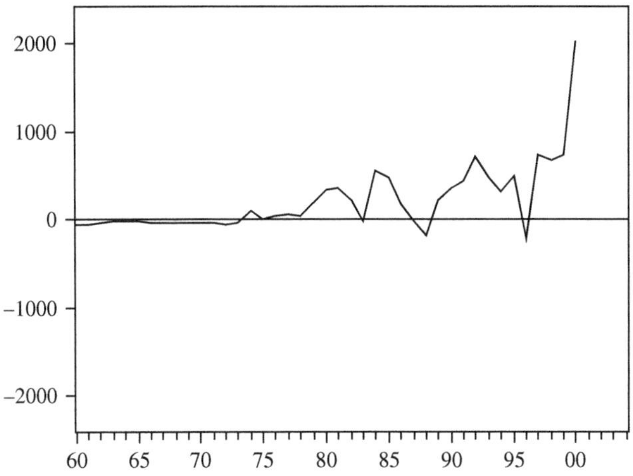

Fig. 8.9. Trade balance (US millions): Republic of the Congo

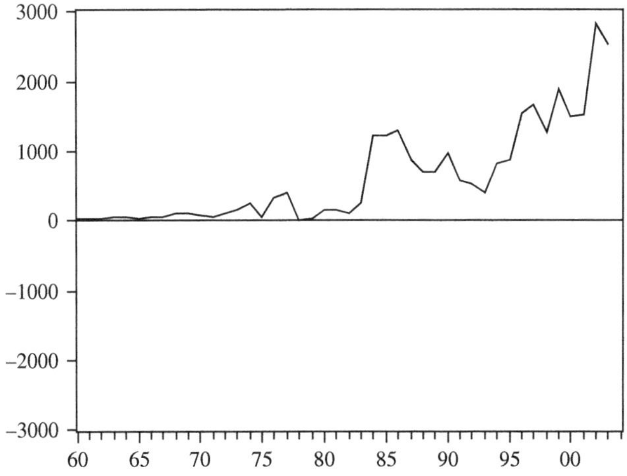

Fig. 8.10. Trade balance (US millions): Côte d'Ivoire

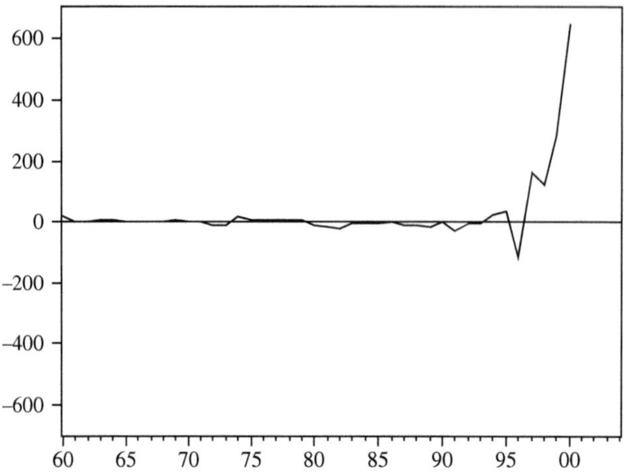

Fig. 8.11. Trade balance (US millions): Equatorial Guinea

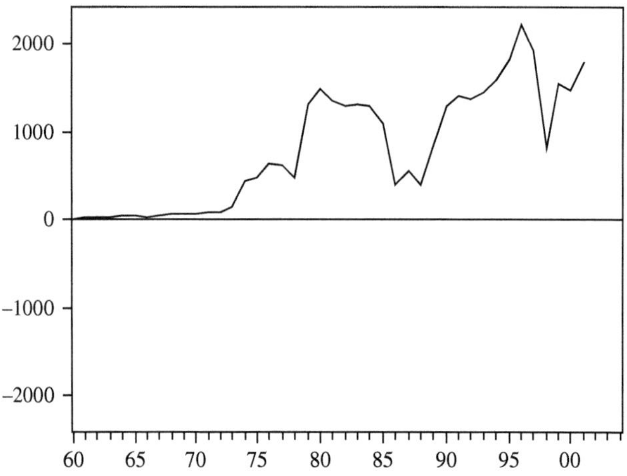

Fig. 8.12. Trade balance (US millions): Gabon

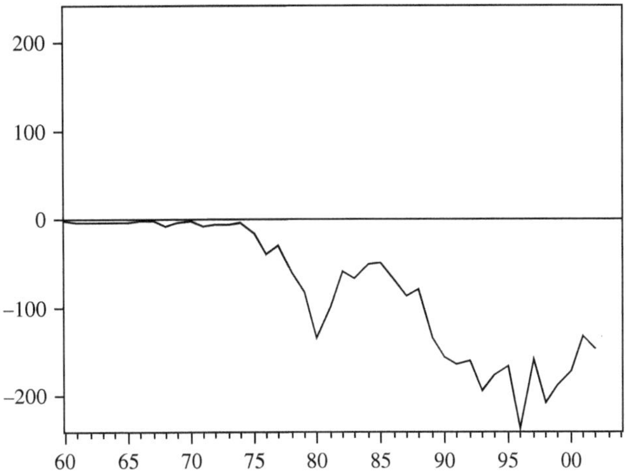

Fig. 8.13. Trade balance (US millions): Gambia

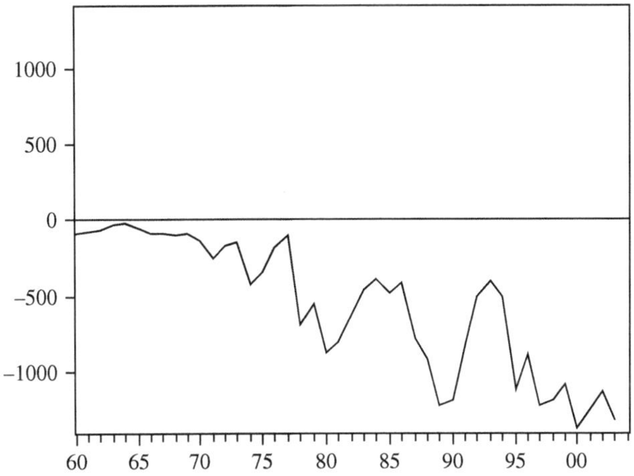

Fig. 8.14. Trade balance (US millions): Kenya

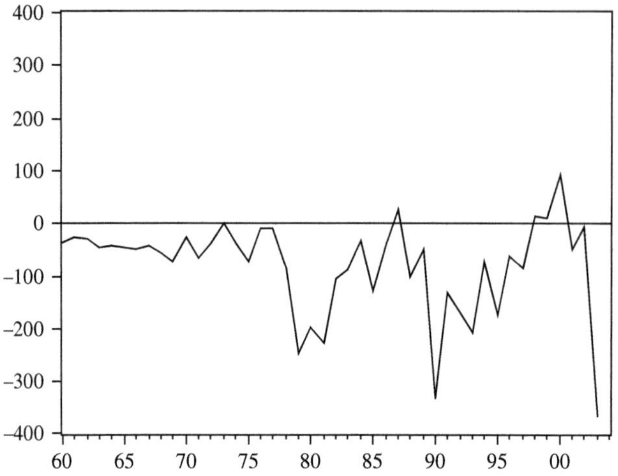

Fig. 8.15. Trade balance (US millions): Madagascar

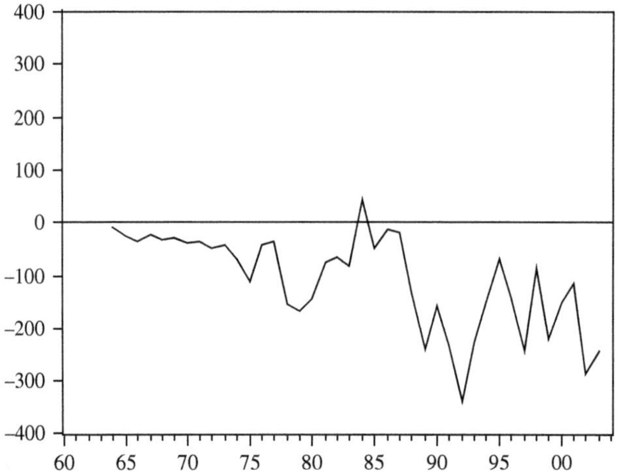

Fig. 8.16. Trade balance (US millions): Malawi

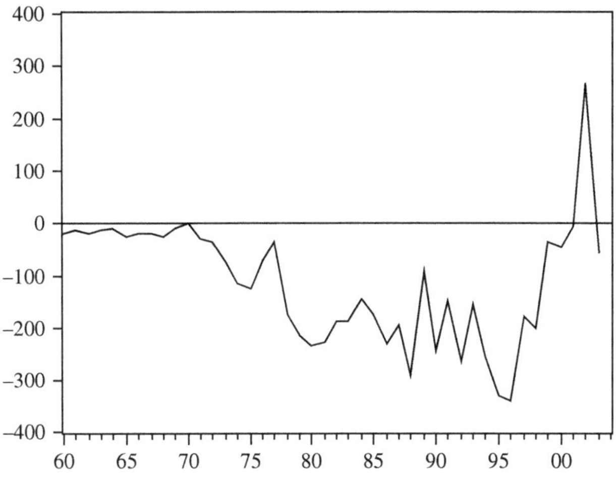

Fig. 8.17. Trade balance (US millions): Mali

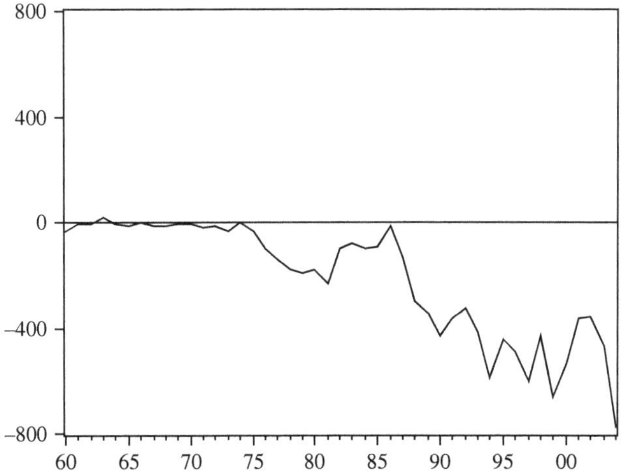

Fig. 8.18. Trade balance (US millions): Mauritius

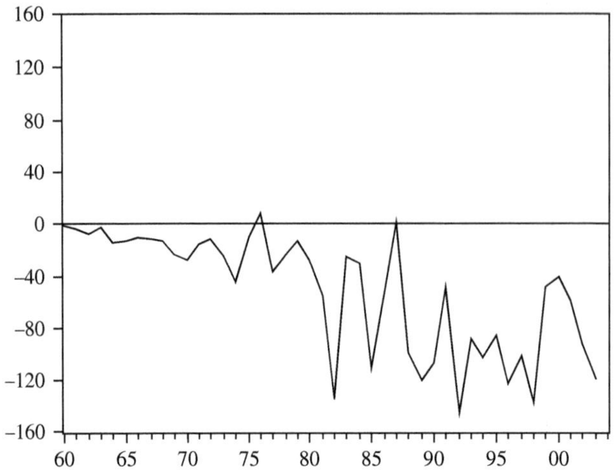

Fig. 8.19. Trade balance (US millions): Niger

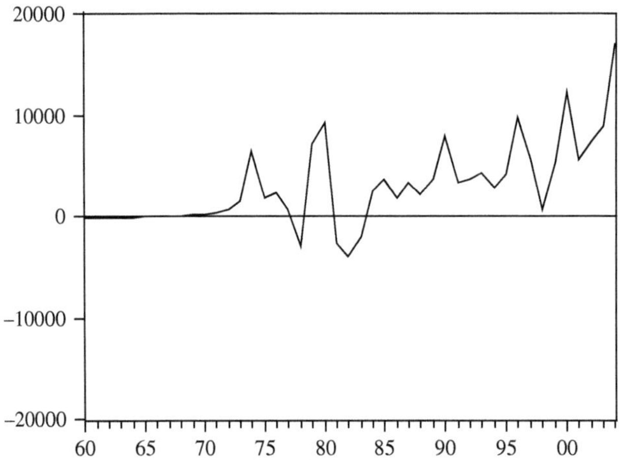

Fig. 8.20. Trade balance (US millions): Nigeria

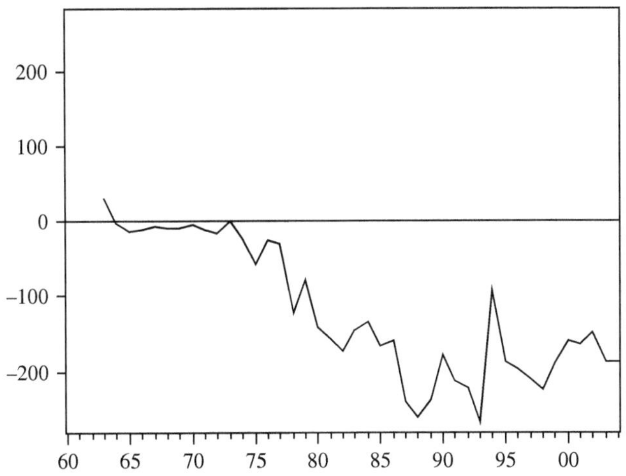

Fig. 8.21. Trade balance (US millions): Rwanda

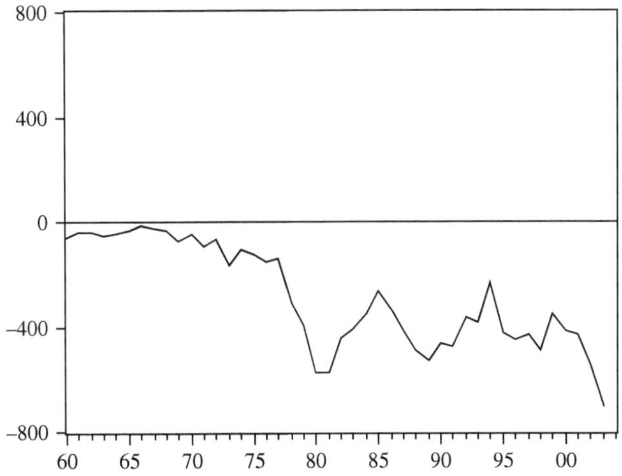

Fig. 8.22. Trade balance (US millions): Senegal

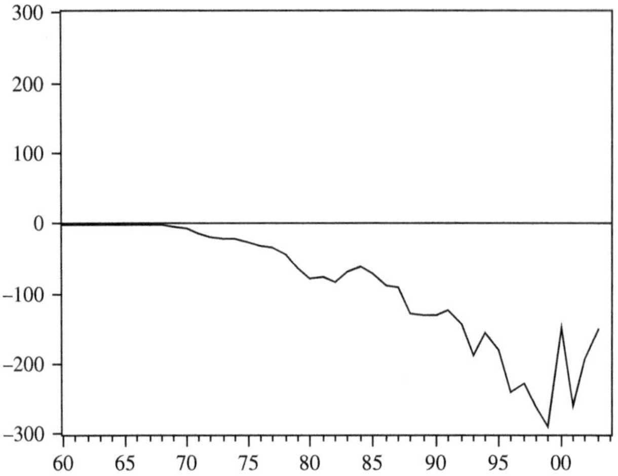

Fig. 8.23. Trade balance (US millions): Seychelles

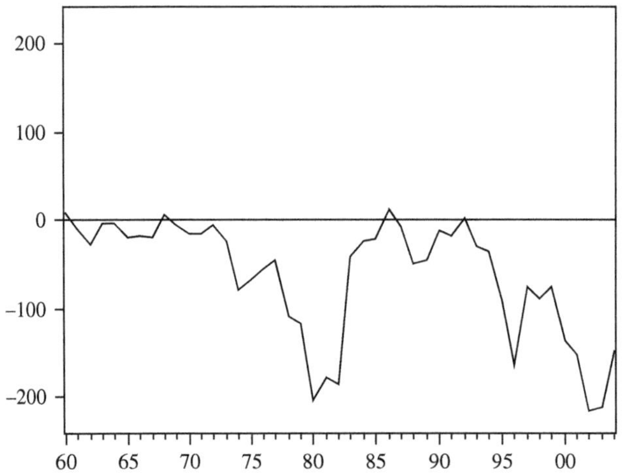

Fig. 8.24. Trade balance (US millions): Sierra Leone

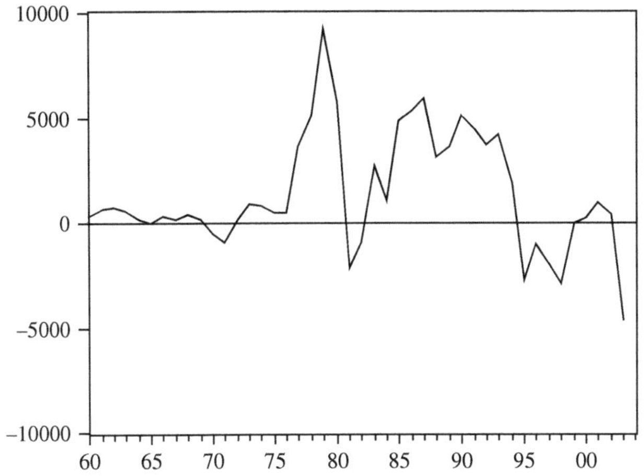

Fig. 8.25. Trade balance (US millions): South Africa

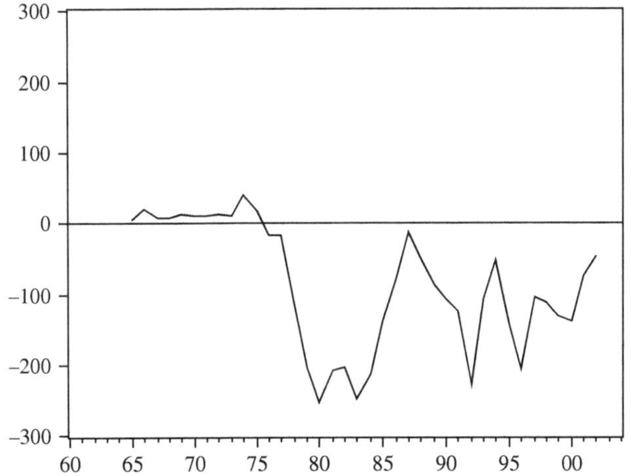

Fig. 8.26. Trade balance (US millions): Swaziland

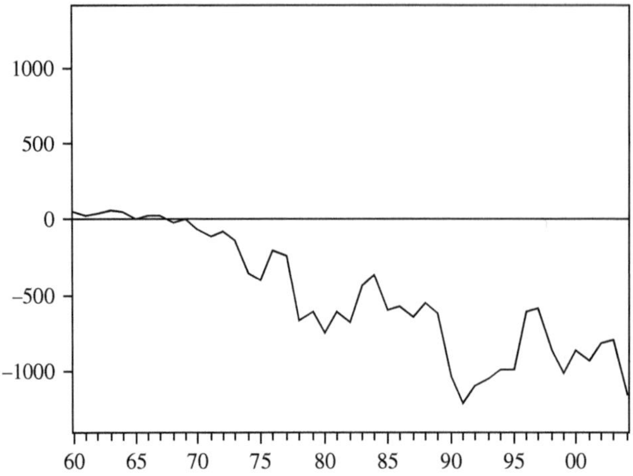

Fig. 8.27. Trade balance (US millions): Tanzania

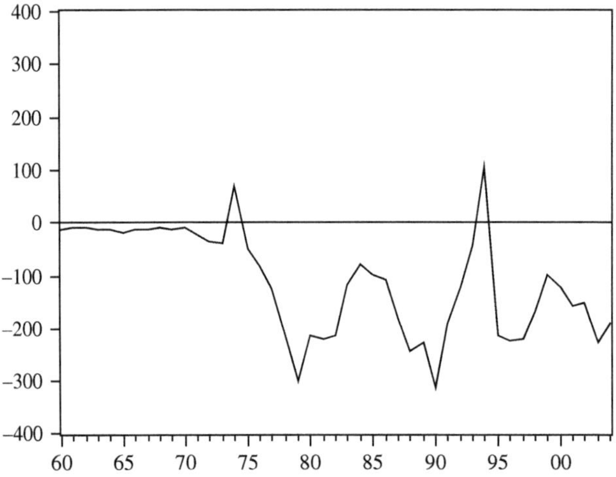

Fig. 8.28. Trade balance (US millions): Togo

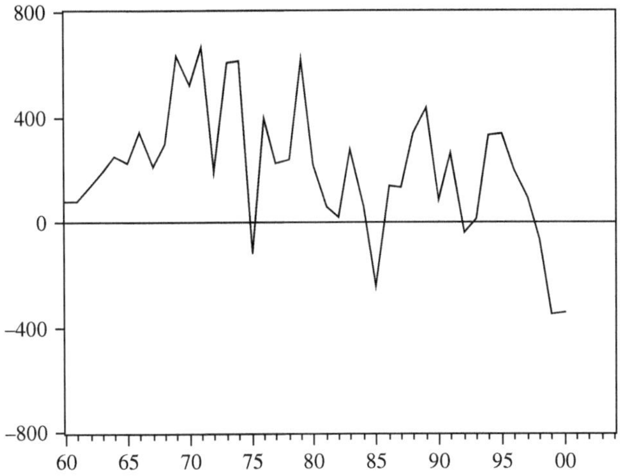

Fig. 8.29. Trade balance (US millions): Zambia

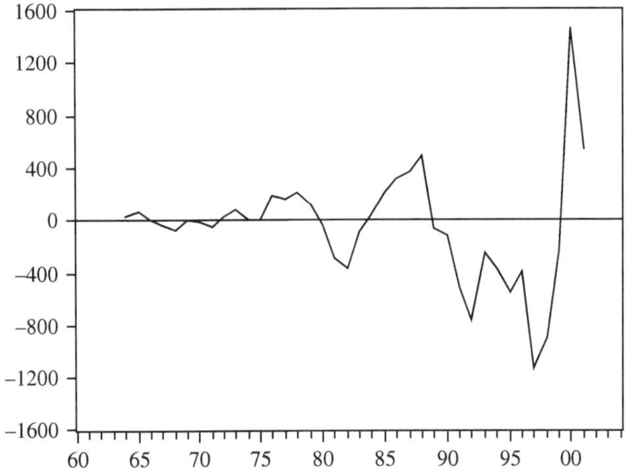

Fig. 8.30. Trade balance (US millions): Zimbabwe

8.4 Empirical Analysis

8.4.1 Panel Unit Root Tests

To begin with, unit root tests must be performed on exports and imports. Here we encounter a problem, however, as the use of annual data alone reduces the sample size for each country. Levin et al. (2002) suggest that individual unit root tests have limited power against alternative hypotheses, especially in small samples. Panel unit root tests help us to overcome this problem. Consider the following AR(1) process for the panel data:

$$y_{i,t} = \rho_i y_{i,t-1} + \delta_i d_{m,t} + \varepsilon_{i,t}, \tag{8.2}$$

where $i = 1, 2, \cdots, N$ are the cross-section series observed over periods $t = 1, 2, \cdots T_i$; ρ_i is an autoregressive coefficient; $d_{m,t}$ is the vector of deterministic variables for model m =1,2,3; δ_i is the corresponding vector of coefficients. Note that $d_{1,t}$={empty set}, $d_{2,t} = \{1\}$ and $d_{3,t} = \{1, t\}$. The errors ε_{it} in (8.2) are assumed to be mutually independent.

Equation (8.2) can be specified as follows:

$$y_{i,t} = \rho_i y_{i,t-1} + \varepsilon_{i,t}, \text{ for } d_{1,t}, \tag{8.2a}$$

$$y_{i,t} = \rho_i y_{i,t-1} + \delta_{0,i} + \varepsilon_{i,t}, \text{ for } d_{2,t}, \tag{8.2b}$$

$$y_{i,t} = \rho_i y_{i,t-1} + \delta_{0,i} + \delta_{1,i} t + \varepsilon_{i,t}, \text{ for } d_{3,t}. \tag{8.2c}$$

Equation (8.2a), (8.2b) and (8.2c) include no deterministic term, individual constant, and individual constant and trend, respectively. If $|\rho_i| < 1$, then y_i is weakly (trend-) stationary. If $\rho_i = 1$, then y_i contains a unit root.

We can make two natural assumptions about ρ_i. First, we can assume that the persistence parameters are common across cross-sections, such that $\rho_i = \rho$ for every i. Levin et al. (2002) make the same assumption. Second, we can allow ρ_i to vary freely across cross-sections. Im et al. (2003) take this approach.

Levin et al. (2002) establish a testing procedure for a common unit root process, such that ρ_i is identical across cross-sections. Levin et al. (2002) employ the following specification:

$$\Delta y_{i,t} = \alpha y_{i,t-1} + \sum_{j=1}^{p_i} \beta_{i,j} \Delta y_{i,t-j} + \delta_i d_{m,t} + \varepsilon_{i,t}, \tag{8.3}$$

where a common $\alpha = \rho - 1$ is assumed but the lag order for the difference terms (p_i) is allowed to vary across cross-sections. The null and alternative hypotheses for the tests can be written thus:

$$H_0 : \alpha = 0,$$

and

$$H_A : \alpha < 0.$$

The null hypothesis holds that each individual time series has a unit root. The alternative hypothesis holds that each time series is stationary.

The test proposed by Levin et al. (2002) is restrictive in the sense that it requires ρ to be homogeneous across i. Im et al. (2003) allow for a heterogeneous coefficient of ρ_i and propose an alternative testing procedure based on the averaging of individual unit root test statistics. They consider a separate ADF regression for each cross section:

$$\Delta y_{i,t} = \alpha_i y_{i,t-1} + \sum_{j=1}^{p_i} \beta_{i,j} \Delta y_{i,t-j} + \delta_i d_{m,t} + \varepsilon_{i,t}. \tag{8.4}$$

The null hypothesis is written as,

$$H_0 : \alpha_i = 0, \text{ for all } i,$$

while the alternative hypothesis is given by:

$$H_A : \begin{cases} \alpha_i = 0, & \text{for } i = 1, 2, \cdots, N_1, \\ \alpha_i < 0, & \text{for } i = N_1 + 1, N_1 + 2, \cdots, N. \end{cases}$$

The null hypothesis holds that each series in the panel has a unit root. The alternative hypothesis allows for some (but not all) of the individual series to have unit roots.[3]

Table 8.2 shows the results of panel unit root tests performed on exports. The table lists the LLC (Levin, Lin, and Chu) statistics, the IPS (Im, Pesaran and Shin) statistics, and their respective p-values. The selection for the number of lags in the regression for cross sections, (8.3) or (8.4), was based on the AIC. We use two types of specification for the deterministic component: one is the individual constant and the other is the individual constant and trends.

Looking first at the results for the entire sample period of 1960-2004, the LLC statistic and its p-value are 2.084 and 0.981 for $d_{3,t}$, and 6.650 and 1.000 for $d_{2,t}$, respectively. The IPS statistic and its p-value are -0.955 and 0.170 for $d_{3,t}$, and 9.128 and 1.000 for $d_{2,t}$, respectively. Thus, the null hypothesis that exports have a unit root is accepted.

[3] In Monte Carlo experiments, Im et al. (2003) show that the small sample properties of IPS test is better than those of the LLC test if a large enough lag order is selected for the underlying ADF regressions.

Table 8.2. Results of panel unit root test: export

Method	Deterministic Term	Test Statistic	*p*-value
[Sample A]: 1960-2004			
LLC	$d_{3,t}$	2.084	0.981
	$d_{2,t}$	6.650	1.000
IPS	$d_{3,t}$	–0.955	0.170
	$d_{2,t}$	9.128	1.000
[Sample B]: 1960-1980			
LLC	$d_{3,t}$	13.415	1.000
	$d_{2,t}$	15.113	1.000
IPS	$d_{3,t}$	9.002	1.000
	$d_{2,t}$	17.395	1.000
[Sample C]: 1981-2004			
LLC	$d_{3,t}$	1.101	0.865
	$d_{2,t}$	3.879	1.000
IPS	$d_{3,t}$	–0.746	0.228
	$d_{2,t}$	4.997	1.000

Note:
Null hypothesis is no unit root.
LLC indicates the Levin, Lin and Chu (2002) test.
IPS indicates the Im, Pesaran and Shin (2003) test.
$d_{3,t}$ indicates the individual effect and individual trend.
$d_{2,t}$ indicates the individual effect.

Next we examine the results when the sample period is divided into two halves, with 1980 as the midpoint. The division of the sample period at this midpoint is presumably meaningful, given that the trade balance of many countries begins to expand in about 1980. Perron (1989) pointed out that researchers often encounter unit roots in analyses performed without considering structural changes. As we clearly see from Table 8.1, however, the null hypothesis that exports have a unit root cannot be rejected for each sub-sample. The result stays the same when the testing method and the specification of the deterministic component are changed.

Table 8.3 shows the results of panel unit root tests performed on imports. With only a few exceptions, these results clearly indicate that imports have a unit root. Here, too, the result stays the same when the testing method, the specification of the deterministic component, and the sample period are changed.

Table 8.3. Results of panel unit root test: import

Method	Deterministic Term	Test Statistic	p-value
[Sample A]: 1960-2004			
LLC	$d_{3,t}$	6.922	1.000
	$d_{2,t}$	5.615	1.000
IPS	$d_{3,t}$	–1.570	0.058
	$d_{2,t}$	6.923	1.000
[Sample B]: 1960-1980			
LLC	$d_{3,t}$	17.097	1.000
	$d_{2,t}$	24.103	1.000
IPS	$d_{3,t}$	14.455	1.000
	$d_{2,t}$	20.241	1.000
[Sample C]: 1981-2004			
LLC	$d_{3,t}$	1.892	0.971
	$d_{2,t}$	2.372	0.991
IPS	$d_{3,t}$	–2.215	0.013
	$d_{2,t}$	1.047	0.852

Note:
Null hypothesis is no unit root.
LLC indicates the Levin, Lin and Chu (2002) test.
IPS indicates the Im, Pesaran and Shin (2003) test.
$d_{3,t}$ indicates the individual effect and individual trend.
$d_{2,t}$ indicates the individual effect.

8.4.2 Panel Cointegration Tests

Lastly, we search for a cointegrating relationship between exports and imports. The trade account, or trade balance, is defined by the following equation:

$$TB_t = EX_t - IM_t = \begin{pmatrix} 1 & -1 \end{pmatrix} \begin{pmatrix} EX_t \\ IM_t \end{pmatrix}, \tag{8.5}$$

where TB_t represents the trade balance at time t, EX_t represents exports at time t, and IM_t represents imports at time t. Consequently, if exports and imports have a cointegrating relationship with a cointegrating vector $(1,-1)$, then $EX_t - IM_t$ becomes a stationary variable and the trade balance also becomes stationary as a result. Husted (1992) pointed out that if an intertemporal budget constraint is satisfied, then exports and imports have a cointegrating relationship with a cointegrating vector $(1,-1)$. It thus follows that testing for a cointegrating relationship between exports and imports under this constraint is effectively the same as testing for unit roots in trade accounts.

Table 8.4 shows the results of panel unit root tests performed on trade balance. If exports and imports have a cointegrating relationship with a cointegrating vector $(1,-1)$, then trade accounts also become stationary. As is clear from the table, trade accounts are non-stationary variables in almost all the cases. This suggests that there is no cointegrating relation between exports and imports with a cointegrating vector $(1,-1)$. The result remains the same when the testing method, specification of the deterministic component, and sample period are changed.

Table 8.4. Results of panel cointegration test: trade balance

Method	Deterministic Term	Test Statistic	*p*-value
[Sample A]: 1960-2004			
LLC	$d_{3,t}$	4.548	1.000
	$d_{2,t}$	5.809	1.000
IPS	$d_{3,t}$	–0.973	0.165
	$d_{2,t}$	4.165	1.000
[Sample B]: 1960-1980			
LLC	$d_{3,t}$	7.771	1.000
	$d_{2,t}$	14.528	1.000
IPS	$d_{3,t}$	6.461	1.000
	$d_{2,t}$	11.906	1.000
[Sample C]: 1981-2004			
LLC	$d_{3,t}$	0.325	0.627
	$d_{2,t}$	1.594	0.945
IPS	$d_{3,t}$	–2.854	0.002
	$d_{2,t}$	–0.920	0.179

Note:
Null hypothesis is no unit root.
LLC indicates the Levin, Lin and Chu (2002) test.
IPS indicates the Im, Pesaran and Shin (2003) test.
$d_{3,t}$ indicates the individual effect and individual trend.
$d_{2,t}$ indicates the individual effect.

8.5 Conclusion

In this chapter we performed tests on changes in the trade accounts of sub-Saharan African countries. As demonstrated earlier by Husted (1992), the trade balance of an economy is a stationary variable when the economy satisfies intertemporal budget constraints. Husted (1992), Arize (2002) and Irandoust and Ericsson (2004) showed that the trade deficit is stationary and that trade account imbalances will converge to a certain equilibrium over the long run in many countries. According to the analyses in this chapter, however, the trade accounts of sub-Saharan African countries are very likely to be non-stationary variables. The stationarity of these variables has important policy implications. If trade accounts are stationary variable, then even short-run trade deficits will not pose significant problems in the long run. But if they are non-stationary variables, policies must be put in place to prevent the trade deficits from expanding. In this case we must try to determine the effective policy for controlling changes in trade accounts. This is a question warranting serious examination.

References

Arize, A.C. (2002) Imports and exports in 50 countries: Tests of cointegration and structural breaks, *International Review of Economics and Finance*, **11**, 101-115.

Baltagi, B.H. (2005) *Econometric Analysis of Panel Data*, 3rd edn. John Wiley & Sons, Chichester.

Engle, R.F. and Granger, C.W.J. (1987) Cointegration and error correction: Representation, estimation and inference, *Econometrica*, **55**, 251-276.

Husted, S. (1992) The emerging U.S. current account deficit in the 1980's: A cointegration analysis, *Review of Economics and Statistics*, **74**, 159-166.

Im, K.S., Pesaran, M.H. and Shin, Y. (2003) Testing for unit roots in heterogeneous panels, *Journal of Econometrics*, **115**, 53-74.

Irandoust, M. and Ericsson, J. (2004) Are imports and exports cointegrated? An international comparison, *Metroeconomica*, **55**, 49-64.

Johansen, S. (1988) Statistical analysis of cointegration vectors, *Journal of Economic Dynamics and Control*, **44**, 215-254.

Johansen, S., and Juselius, K. (1990) Maximum likelihood estimation and inference on cointegration with application to the demand for money, *Oxford Bulletin of Economics and Statistics*, **52**, 169-209.

Levin, A., Lin, C.F. and Chu, C. (2002) Unit root tests in panel data: Asymptotic and finite-sample properties, *Journal of Econometrics*, **108**, 1-24.

Mann, C.L. (2002) Perspective on the U.S. current account deficit and sustainability, *Journal of Economic Perspective*, **16**, 131-152.

Perron, P. (1989) The great crash, the oil price shock, and the unit root hypothesis, *Econometrica*, **57**, 1361-1401.

Phillips, P.C.B. and Moon, H.R. (2000) Nonstationary panel data analysis: an overview of some recent developments, *Econometric Reviews*, **19**, 263-286.

9 Trade Balance and the Terms of Trade

9.1 Introduction

Changes in the exchange rate impact the trade balance by changing the terms of trade. The relationship between terms of trade and the trade balance is ordinarily analyzed using the Marshall-Lerner condition (ML condition). The ML condition holds that deterioration in the terms of trade is to improve a country's trade balance, provided that the sum of the country's price elasticity of demand for exports and imports must be greater than one in absolute value. The principle is named after the economists Alfred Marshall and Abba Lerner. As a devaluation of the exchange rate reduces the price of exports, the demand for exports will increase. The price of imports, meanwhile, will rise, and the demand for imports will decrease. The net effect on the trade balance will depend on price elasticities. If exported goods are elastic to price, their demand will increase proportionately more than the decrease in price, and the total export revenue will increase. If imported goods are elastic, the total import expenditure will decrease. The trade balance will improve in both cases (Fig. 9.1).

To check the ML condition using actual data, it is necessary to estimate both the import function and the export function. Such an approach has been taken in past research, i.e. Arize (1990), Goldstein and Khan (1978), Houthakker and Magee (1969), and Warner and Kreinin (1983). In such research, it was reported that the ML condition was fulfilled. However, there

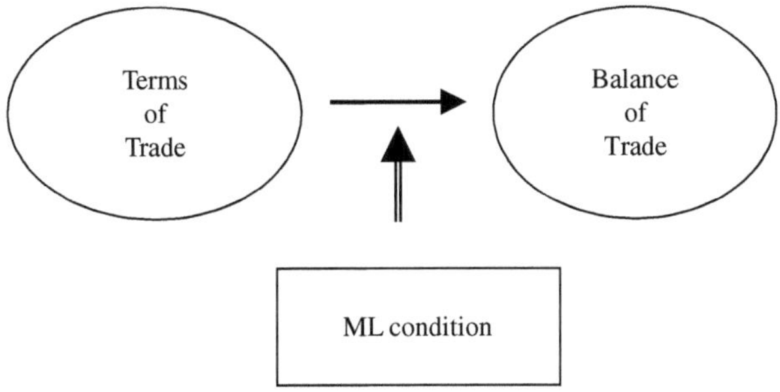

Fig. 9.1. Marshall-Lerner condition

is a problem with this approach. In order to estimate the export function and the import function, it is necessary to collect data such as world income, world export prices and effective exchange rates, and to specify trading partners. For many countries, however, it is difficult to collect such data.

Haynes and Stone (1982) attempt to address this issue by directly analyzing the relationship between the trade balance and terms of trade – an alternative approach. They analyze the impact of terms of trade on the trade balance by looking at the estimated coefficients of terms of trade using a distributed lag model. Haynes and Stone (1982), on the other hand, conduct their analysis within the framework of regression analysis and are thus unable to avoid the spurious regression of Granger and Newbold (1974).

With the recent development of time series analysis, cointegration analysis is now used for analyzing long-run relationships among variables. Arize (1996) uses cointegration analysis to empirically analyze the long-run equilibrium between the trade balance and the terms of trade using quarterly data on sixteen countries from 1973 to 1992, i.e. the G7 members (Canada, France, Germany, Italy, Japan, the United Kingdom, the United States), Denmark, Finland, the Netherlands, Switzerland, and five newly industrializing economies (NIES: India, Korea, Malaysia, Mexico, Sri Lanka). Arize (1996) reports a long-run relationship between the trade balance and the terms of trade in many countries.

This chapter expands on this Arize (1996) analysis by empirically analyzing the relationship between the trade balance and the terms of trade in sub-Saharan African countries. A distinctive feature of this research is the use of panel unit root and panel cointegration analysis, an approach not attempted by Arize (1996). With many of the sub-Saharan African countries, the only data available are annual and the samples sizes are small. The individual nonstationary time series analysis is known to have low power for short span of the data. We pool the data of sub-Saharan countries in the hopes of adding cross-sectional variation to the data that will increase the power of panel unit root or panel cointegration tests.

9.2 Basic Model

Following Haynes and Stone (1982) and Arize (1996), we can write the long-run relationship between the trade balance and the terms of trade as follows:

$$TB_t = \alpha + \beta TOT_t + u_t, \qquad (9.1)$$

where TB_t is the trade balance at time t, TOT_t is the terms of trade at time t, and u_t is a disturbance at time t. If trade balance and terms of trade are cointegrated, they have a long-run equilibrium relationship. If the ML condition is satisfied in the long-run, then an increase in the terms of trade can be expected to increase the trade balance, and thus $\beta > 0$.

9.3 Data

This chapter analyzes 19 sub-Saharan African countries using annual data for the period between 1970 and 2004: Benin; Burkina Faso; Cameroon, Chad; Republic of the Congo; Côte d'Ivoire; Gabon; Ghana; Guinea-Bissau; Kenya; Madagascar; Malawi; Mali; Nigeria; Rwanda; Senegal; South Africa; Togo; Zambia. The data were obtained from the World Development Indicators (The World Bank). The real trade balance and terms of trade are used for the empirical analysis. The real trade balance is obtained as follows: exports of goods and services (in constant local currency unit) minus imports of goods and services (in constant local currency unit). Note that the real trade balance is measured as a share of real GDP for empirical analysis. The terms of trade are obtained as a ratio of export prices to import prices in the local currency unit. The data are balanced panel data without any missing observations.

Figures 9.2a through 9.20b show the movements of the trade balance and the terms of trade for each country. These figures suggest that the trade balance and the terms of trend may move together and thus may have a cointegrating relation in many of the countries.

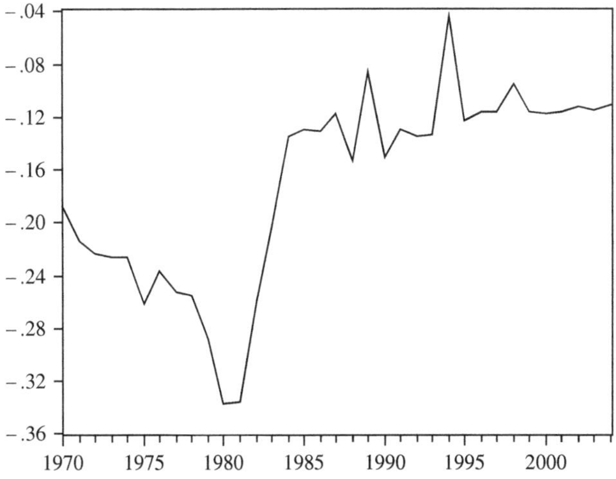

Fig. 9.2a. Trade balance: Benin

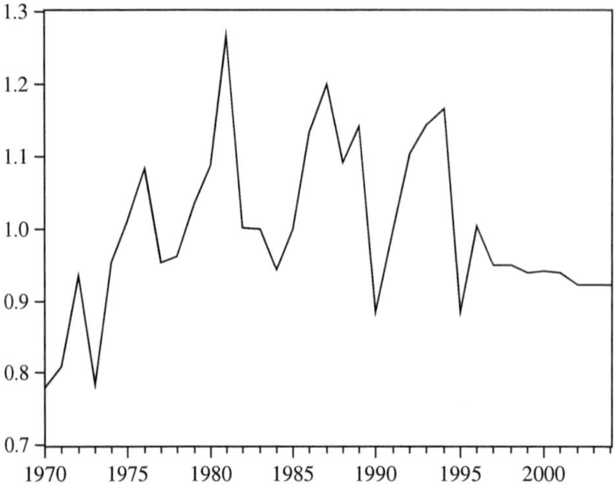

Fig. 9.2b. Terms of trade: Benin

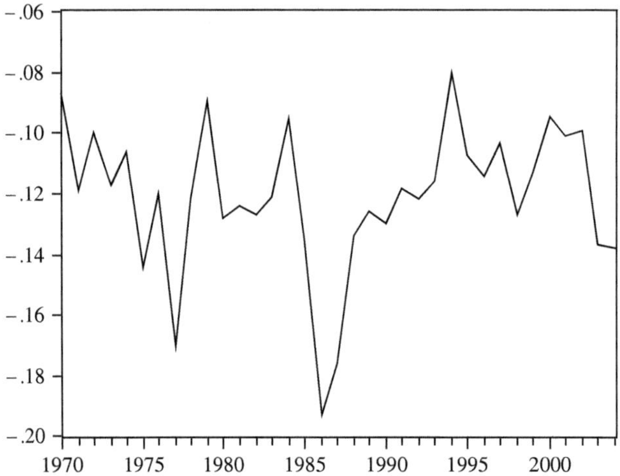

Fig. 9.3a. Trade balance: Burkina Faso

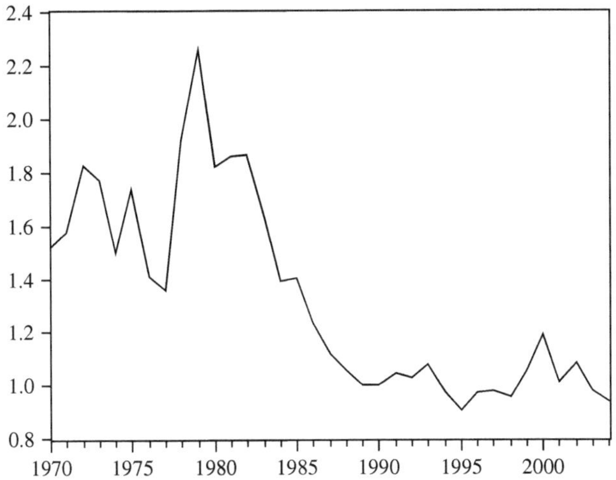

Fig. 9.3b. Terms of trade: Burkina Faso

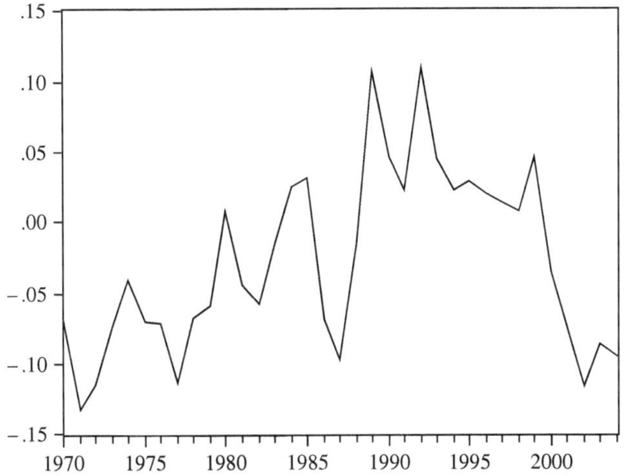

Fig. 9.4a. Trade balance: Cameroon

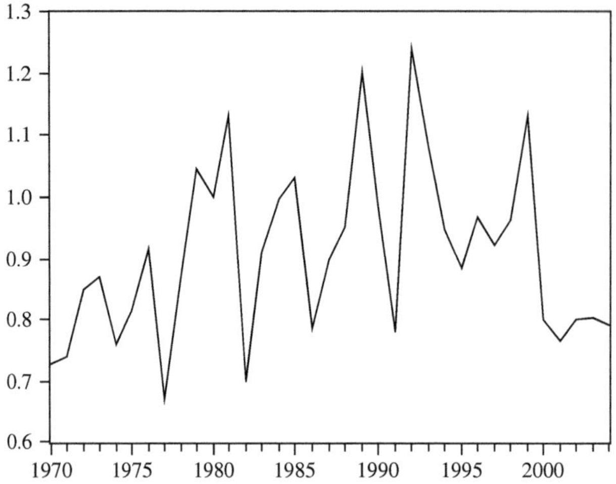

Fig. 9.4b. Terms of trade: Cameroon

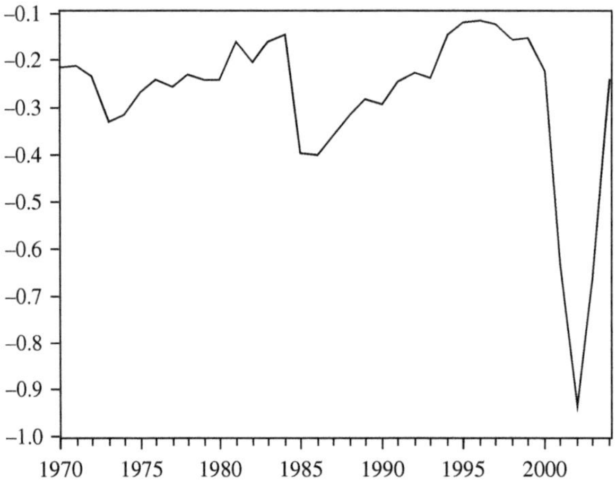

Fig. 9.5a. Trade balance: Chad

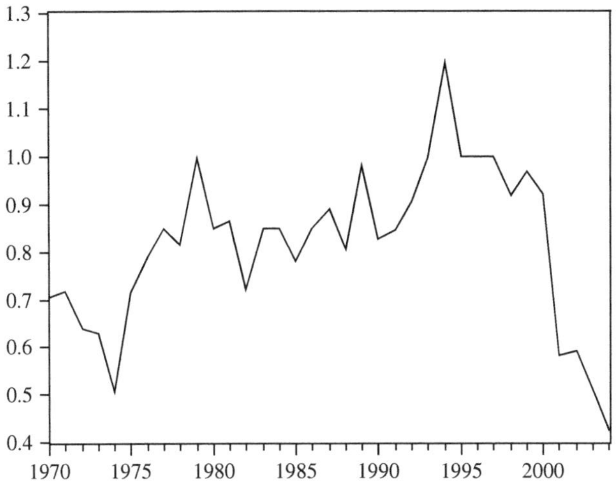

Fig. 9.5b. Terms of trade: Chad

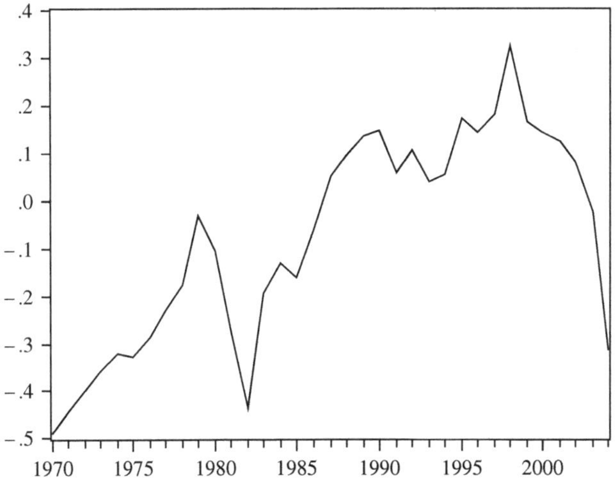

Fig. 9.6a. Trade balance: Republic of the Congo

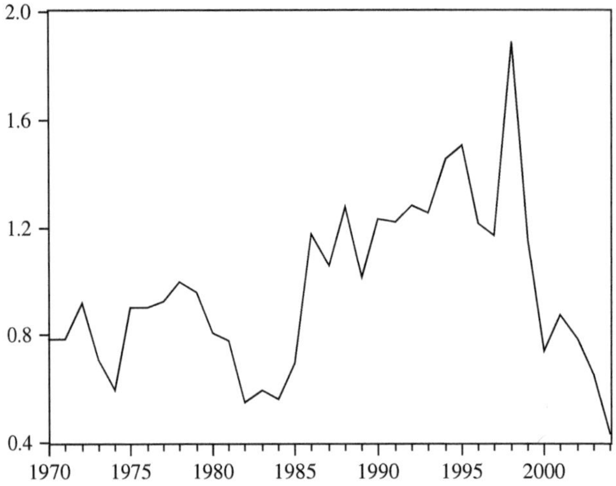

Fig. 9.6b. Terms of trade: Republic of the Congo

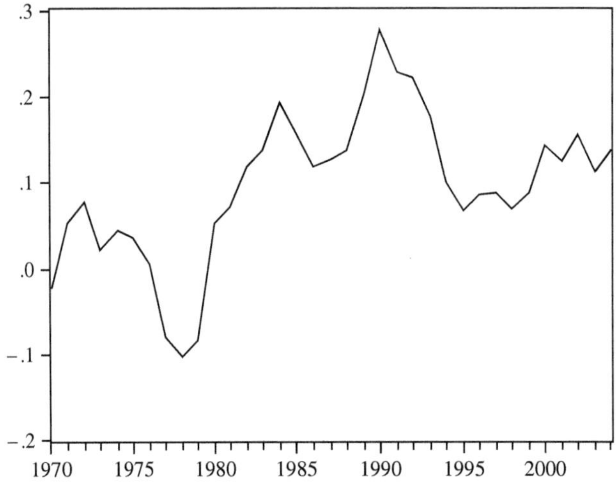

Fig. 9.7a. Trade balance: Côte d'Ivoire

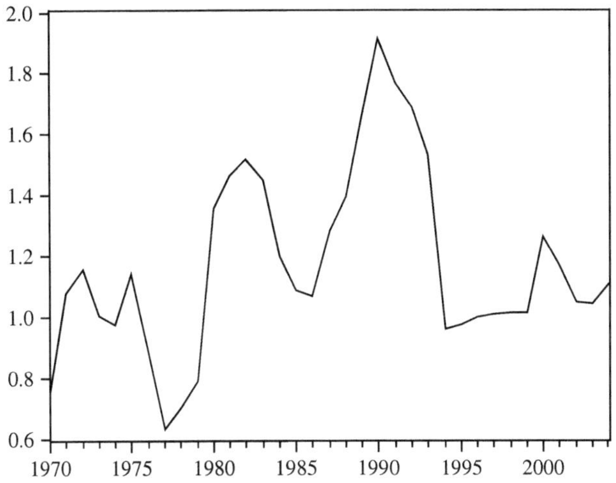

Fig. 9.7b. Terms of trade: Côte d'Ivoire

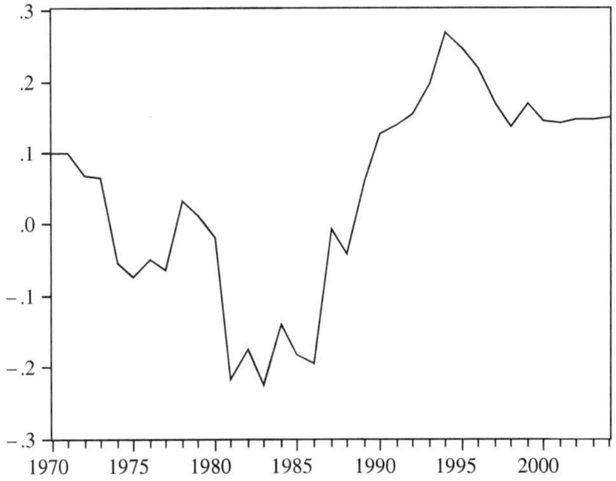

Fig. 9.8a. Trade balance: Gabon

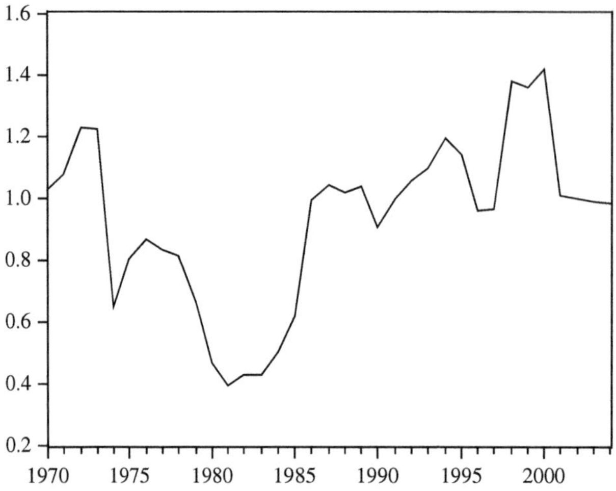

Fig. 9.8b. Terms of trade: Gabon

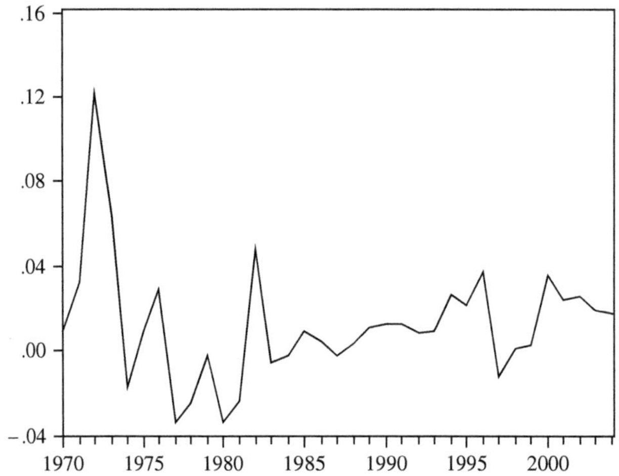

Fig. 9.9a. Trade balance: Ghana

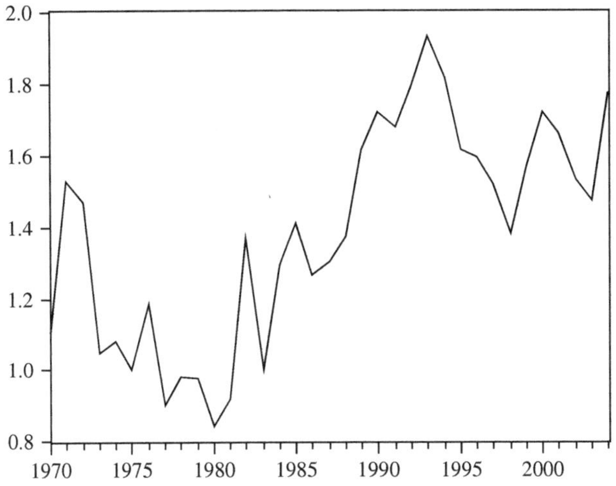

Fig. 9.9b. Terms of trade: Ghana

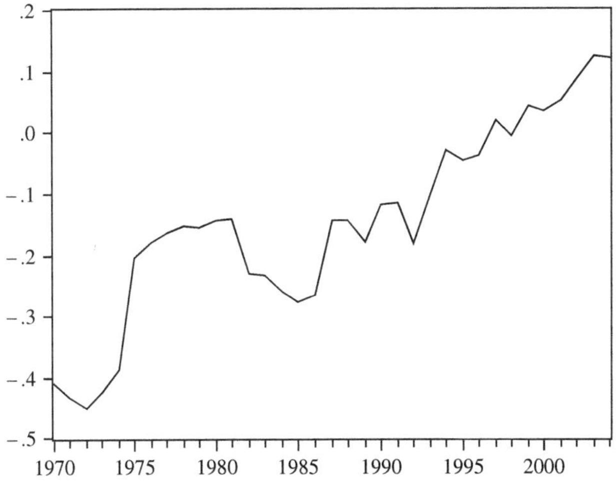

Fig. 9.10a. Trade balance: Guinea-Bissau

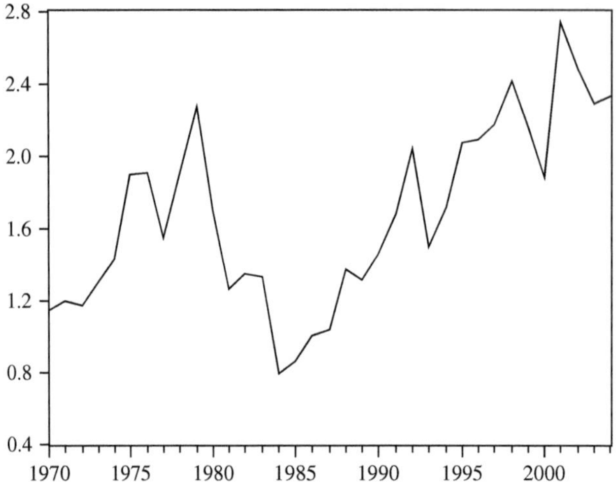

Fig. 9.10b. Terms of trade: Guinea-Bissau

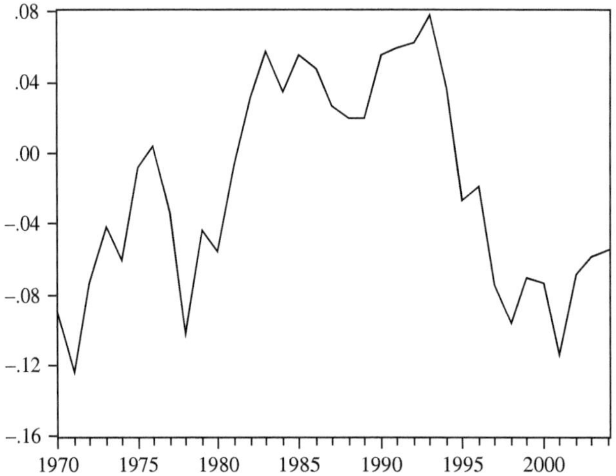

Fig. 9.11a. Trade balance: Kenya

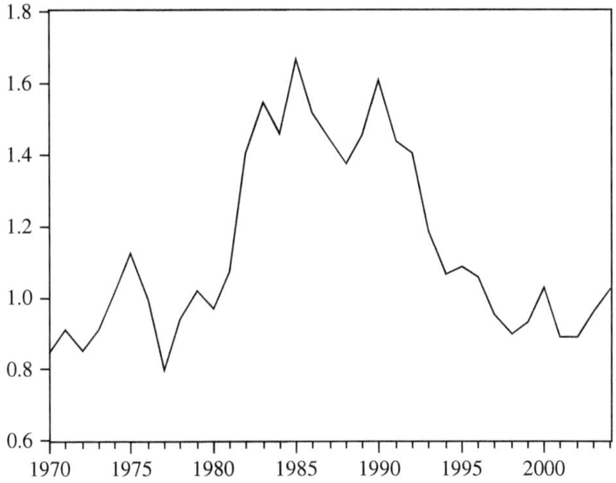

Fig. 9.11b. Terms of trade: Kenya

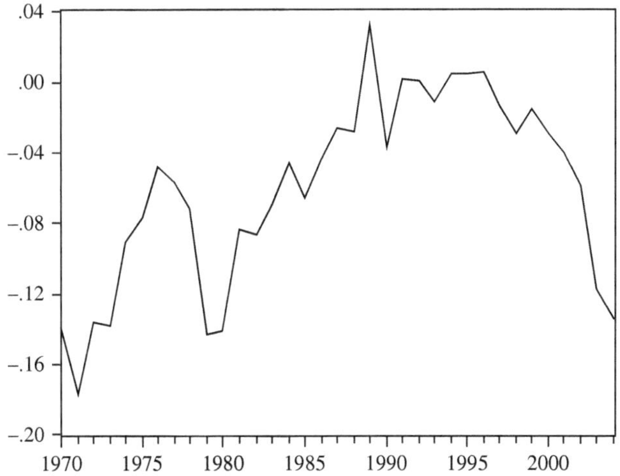

Fig. 9.12a. Trade balance: Madagascar

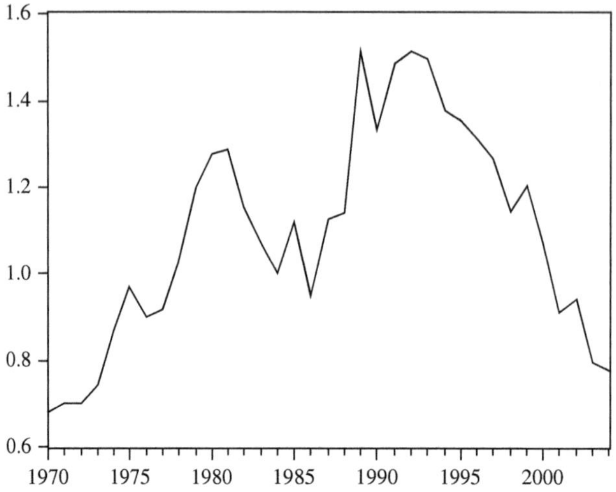

Fig. 9.12b. Terms of trade: Madagascar

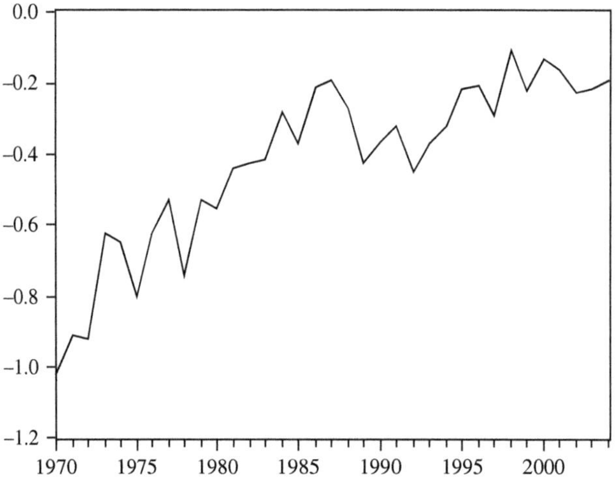

Fig. 9.13a. Trade balance: Malawi

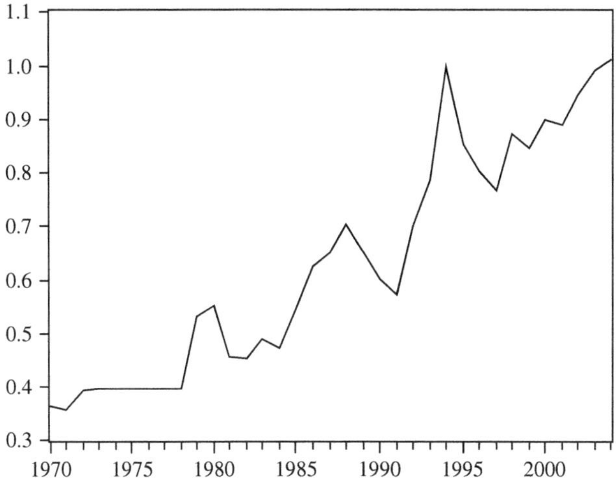

Fig. 9.13b. Terms of trade: Malawi

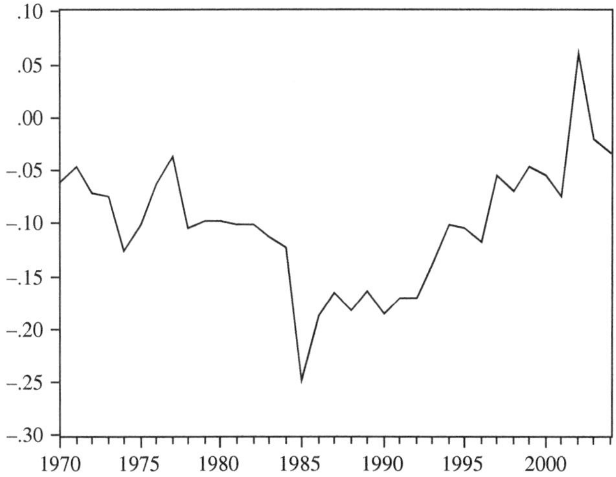

Fig. 9.14a. Trade balance: Mali

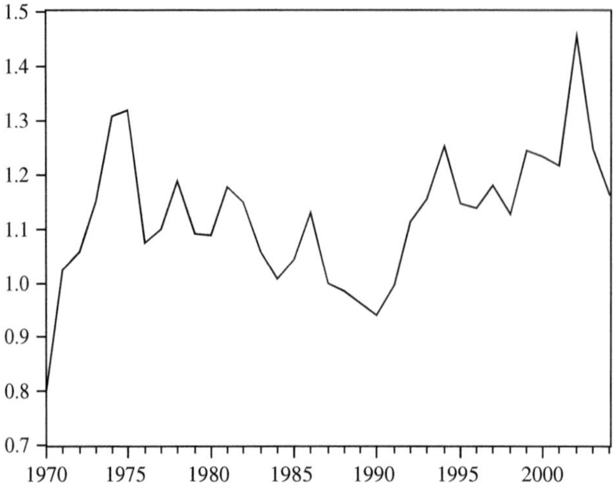

Fig. 9.14b. Terms of trade: Mali

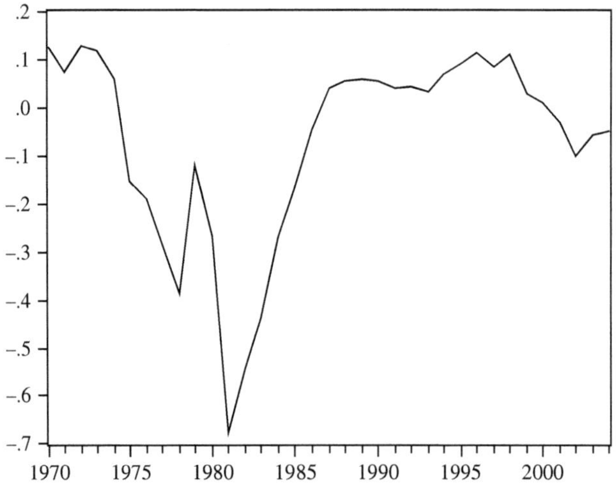

Fig. 9.15a. Trade balance: Nigeria

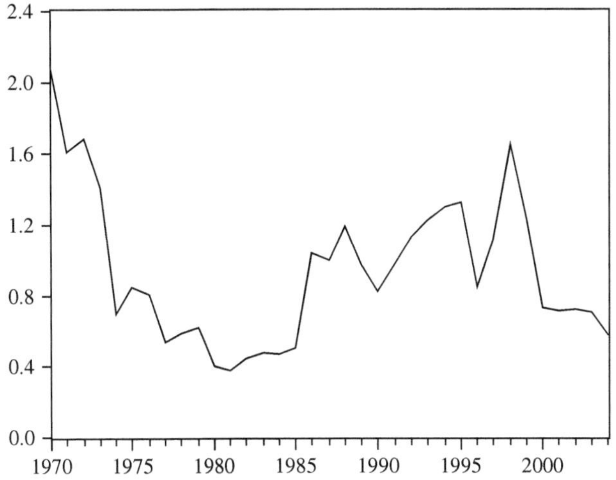

Fig. 9.15b. Terms of trade: Nigeria

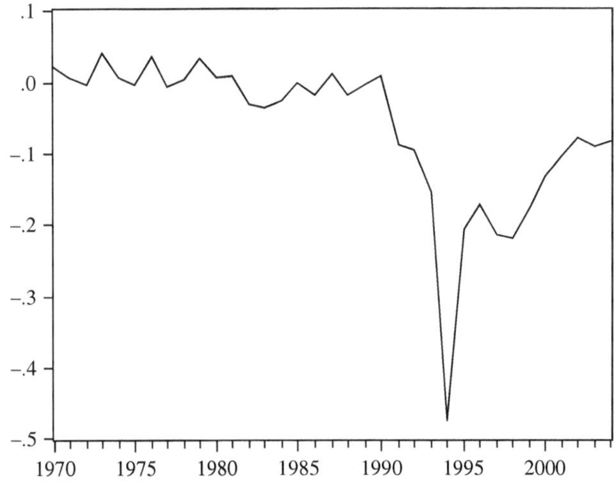

Fig. 9.16a. Trade balance: Rwanda

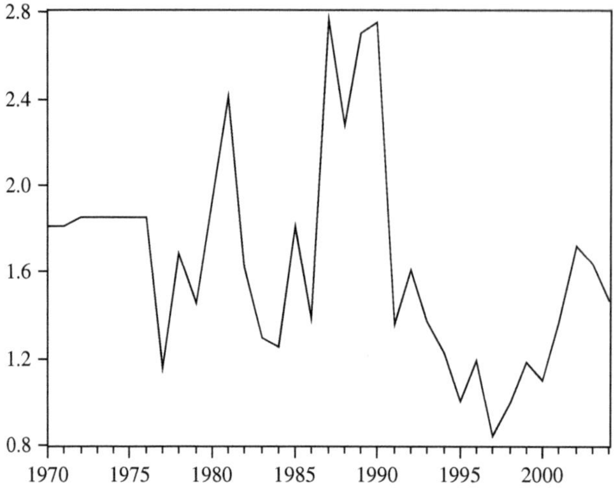

Fig. 9.16b. Terms of trade: Rwanda

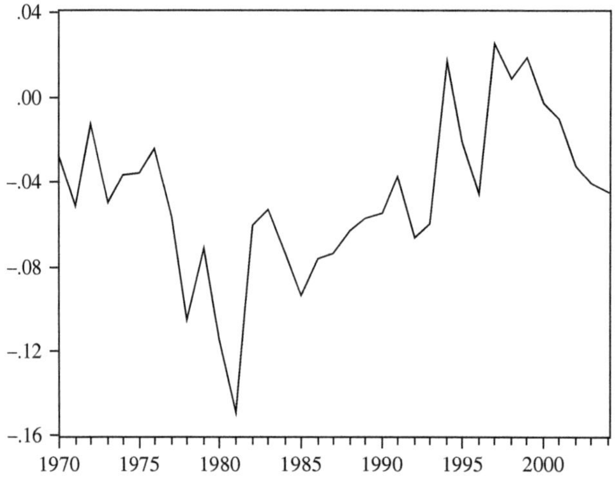

Fig. 9.17a. Trade balance: Senegal

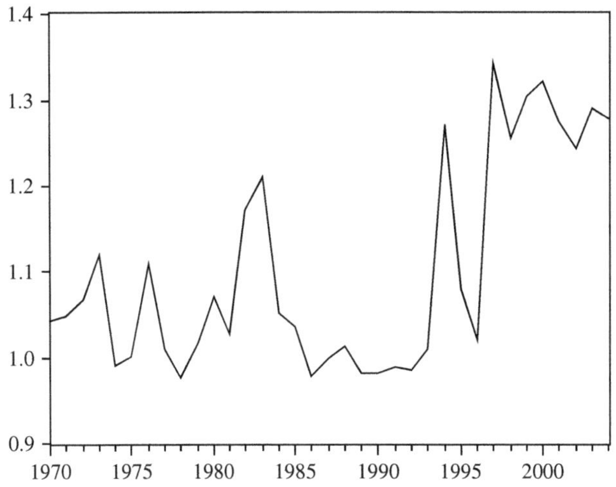

Fig. 9.17b. Terms of trade: Senegal

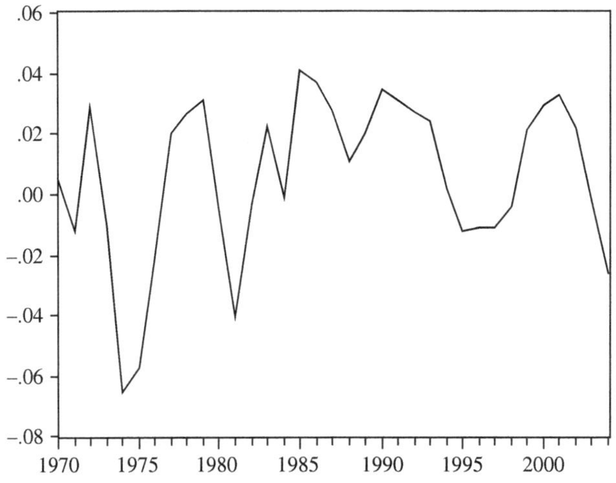

Fig. 9.18a. Trade balance: South Africa

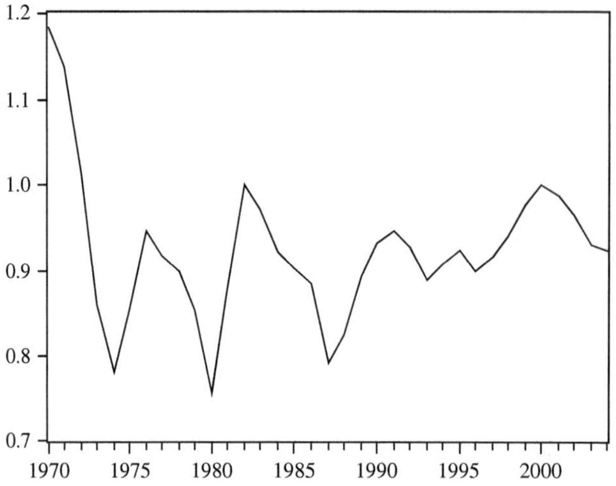

Fig. 9.18b. Terms of trade: South Africa

Fig. 9.19a. Trade balance: Togo

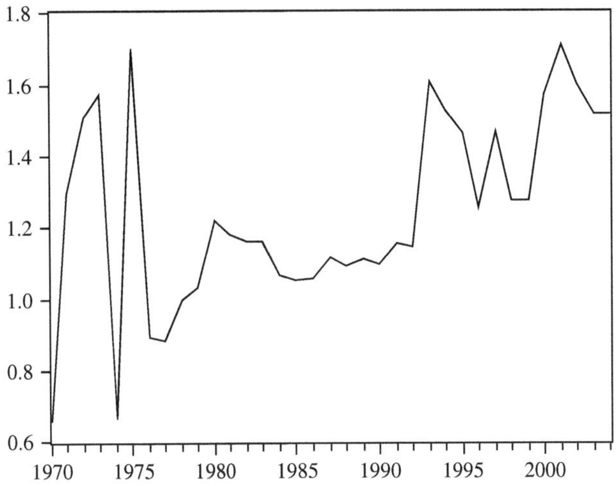

Fig. 9.19b. Terms of trade: Togo

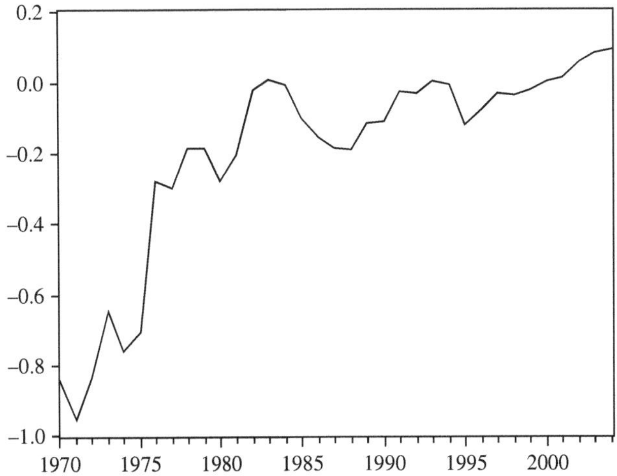

Fig. 9.20a. Trade balance: Zambia

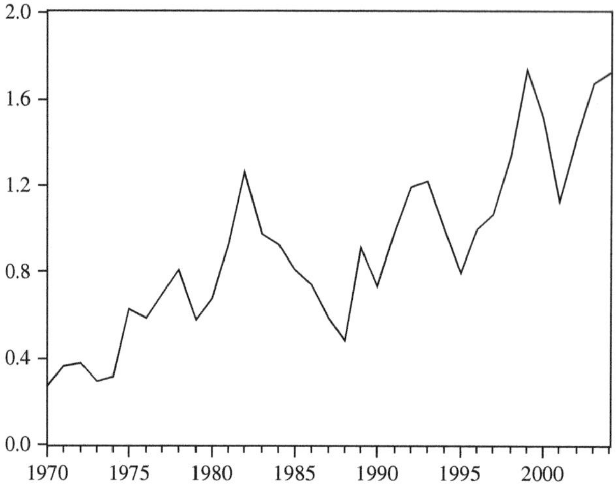

Fig. 9.20b. Terms of trade: Zambia

9.4 Empirical Analysis

9.4.1 Panel Unit Root Tests

To begin with, we need to perform unit root tests on the trade balance and the terms of trade. In doing so, however, the use of annual data in this study forces us to work with fairly small sample sizes for each country. Levin et al. (2002) suggest that individual unit root tests have limited power against alternative hypotheses, especially in small samples. Panel unit root tests help us to overcome the problem.[1]

We use two types of panel unit root tests for empirical analysis. One is the LLC test proposed by Levin et al. (2002) and the other is the Breitung test developed by Breitung (2000). Breitung (2000) finds that the LLC test suffers from a substantial loss of power if individual-specific trends are included, and proposes a test statistic whose power is substantially higher than that of LLC.

For LLC and Breitung tests, we use the following specification:

$$\Delta y_{i,t} = \alpha y_{i,t-1} + \sum_{j=1}^{p_i} \beta_{i,j} \Delta y_{i,t-j} + \delta_{0,i} + \delta_{1,i} t + \varepsilon_{i,t}, \tag{9.2}$$

[1] Phillips and Moon (2000) and Baltagi (2005, Chap. 12) are good reference for nonstationary panel data analysis.

where $i = 1, 2, \cdots, N$ are the cross-section series observed over periods $t = 1, 2, \cdots T_i$; $\delta_{0,i}$ are fixed effects, $\delta_{1,i}t$ are individual time trends; Δ is the difference operator, i.e. $\Delta y_{i,t} = y_{i,t} - y_{i,t-1}$; and the errors ε_{it} are assumed to be mutually independent disturbances.

The null and alternative hypotheses for the tests can be written as:

$$H_0 : \alpha = 0,$$

and

$$H_A : \alpha < 0.$$

The null hypothesis holds that each individual time series has a unit root. The alternative hypothesis holds that each time series is stationary.

Table 9.1 shows the results of panel unit root tests. The LLC test statistics, the Breitung test statistics, and their respective p-values are included. The AIC was used as the criterion for selecting the number of lags (p_i) in (9.2). Individual constant and time trend are used for the deterministic component.

Table 9.1. Results of panel unit root tests

Variable	Method	Test Statistic	p-value
TB_t	LLC test	1.667	0.952
	Breitung test	–0.493	0.311
TOT_t	LLC test	–1.215	0.112
	Breitung test	–0.884	0.189
ΔTB_t	LLC test	–9.202	0.000
	Breitung test	–7.153	0.000
ΔTOT_t	LLC test	–10.679	0.000
	Breitung test	–10.868	0.000

Note:
Null hypothesis is no unit root.
LLC test indicates the Levin, Lin and Chu (2002) test.
Breitung test indicates the Breitung (2000) test.
Δ is the difference operator, i.e. $\Delta y_t = y_t - y_{t-1}$.

From the results in Table 9.1, we find that the LLC test statistic and its p-value are 1.667 and 0.952 for the level of trade balance, and -9.202 and 0.000 for the first difference of trade balance. We obtain the similar results when we use the Breitung test. Thus, the trade balance has a unit root.

Table 9.1 also shows the results of panel unit root tests performed on the terms of trade. The results indicate that the LLC test statistic and its p-value are -1.215 and 0.112 for the level of the terms of trade, and -10.679 and 0.000 for the first difference of the terms of trade. Here too, we obtain the similar results for the Breitung test. Thus, the terms of trade has a unit root as well.

Thus, we can say that the trade balance and the terms of trade are non-stationary variables.

9.4.2 Panel Cointegration Tests

The two series were unable to reject the null of the unit root. Our next step, therefore, is to perform the cointegration test. We start with the following equation:

$$TB_{i,t} = \alpha_i + \beta_i TOT_{i,t} + u_{i,t},\ i = 1,2,\cdots,N,\ t = 1,2,\cdots,T. \tag{9.3}$$

In a bivariate context, Pedroni (1999) develops asymptotic and finite-sample properties of the test statistic to test the null hypothesis of no-cointegration in the panel. While both the homogeneous and heterogeneous panel models are possible, the heterogeneous model such as (9.3) is consistent with the class of model when parameters α and β are allowed to vary across countries. Having no reason to believe that all of the parameters are the same across countries, as is assumed in the homogeneous model, we thus decided to employ the heterogeneous model in our analysis.

Pedroni (1999) derives the asymptotic distribution and explores the small sample performances of seven different statistics. Of these seven statistics, four are based on pooling along what is commonly referred to as the "within-dimension" and three are based on pooling along what is commonly referred to as the "between-dimension." Pedroni (1999) describes the former as "panel cointegration statistics" and the latter as "group mean panel cointegration statistics."

The first of the simple panel cointegration statistics, the "panel v-statistic," is a non-parametric variance ratio statistic. The second, the "panel ρ-statistic," is a panel version of a non-parametric statistic analogous to the familiar Phillips and Perron ρ-statistic. The third, the "panel

t-statistic (non-parametric)," is a non-parametric statistic analogous to the Phillips and Perron t-statistic. The fourth of these simple panel cointegration statistics, the "panel t – statistic (parametric)," is a parametric statistic analogous to the familiar augmented Dickey-Fuller t-statistic.[2]

The other three panel cointegration statistics are based on a group mean approach. The first, the "group ρ-statistic," is analogous to the Phillips and Perron ρ-statistic. The last two, the "group t-statistic (non-parametric) and group t-statistic (parametric)," are analogous to the Phillips and Perron t-statistic and the augmented Dickey-Fuller t-statistic, respectively.

The following four steps must be taken in all cases, regardless of the statistic we choose to construct.

(Step 1) Compute the residuals $\hat{u}_{it}$ of the panel regression in (9.3) after incorporating all the desired terms such as fixed effects or the time trend.

(Step 2) Compute the residuals $\hat{\eta}_{it}$ of the following differenced regression:

$$\Delta TB_{i,t} = \beta_i \Delta TOT_{i,t} + \eta_{i,t}. \tag{9.4}$$

(Step 3) Calculate the long-run variance of $\hat{\eta}_{i,t}$ using a kernel estimator such as the Newey-West (1987) estimator.

(Step 4) Estimate the appropriate autoregression using the residuals $\hat{u}_{it}$ of the original cointegrating regression, choosing either of the following forms (a) or (b):

(a) For the non-parametric statistics, estimate

$$\hat{u}_{i,t} = \gamma_i \hat{u}_{i,t-1} + v_{i,t}, \tag{9.5}$$

and use the residuals to compute the long-run variance of $v_{i,t}$.

(b) For the parametric case, estimate

$$\hat{u}_{i,t} = \gamma_i \hat{u}_{i,t-1} + \sum_{k=1}^{K_i} \delta_{i,k} \Delta \hat{u}_{i,t-k} + w_{i,t}, \tag{9.6}$$

and use the residuals to compute the simple variance of w_{it}.

By taking these four steps we can construct seven test statistics. Next, we normalize these statistics by the appropriate mean and variance adjustment terms reported in Pedroni's Table 2 (Pedroni, 1999, p.666) so that the appropriate tails of the normal distribution can be used to judge their significance.

[2] See Table 1 of Pedroni (1999, p.660).

The within-dimension statistics are based on estimators that effectively pool the autoregressive coefficient across different members for the unit root tests on the estimated residuals. The between-dimension statistics are based on estimators that simply average the individually estimated coefficients for each member i. A consequence of this distribution arises in terms of the autoregressive coefficient, γ_i, of the estimated residuals (9.5) or (9.6) under the alternative hypothesis of cointegration.

The null and alternative hypotheses for the within-dimension statistics are given by,

$$H_0 : \gamma_i = 1 \text{ for all } i,$$

and

$$H_1 : \gamma_i = \gamma < 1 \text{ for all } i,$$

where the alternative hypothesis presumes a common value for $\gamma_i = \gamma$.

In contrast, the null and alternative hypotheses for the between-dimension statistics are given by,

$$H_0 : \gamma_i = 1 \text{ for all } i,$$

and

$$H_1 : \gamma_i < 1 \text{ for all } i,$$

where the alternative hypothesis does not presume a common value for $\gamma_i = \gamma$. Thus, the between-dimension-based statistics allow the modeling of an additional source of potential heterogeneity across individual members of the panel.

Table 9.2 shows the results of panel unit cointegration tests on the trade balance and the terms of trade. The test statistics are as follows: 3.297 for the panel ν-statistic, -6.035 for the panel ρ-statistic, -5.875 for the non-parametric panel t-statistic, -5.646 for the parametric panel t-statistic, -4.081 for the group ρ-statistic, -5.574 for the non-parametric group t-statistic, and -5.626 for the parametric group t-statistic. This table clearly indicates that the null hypothesis of no cointegration is rejected for every case considered. Thus, the trade balance and the terms of trade are cointegrated in sub-Saharan African countries.

Table 9.2. Results of panel cointegration test

Method	Test Statistic
Panel ν -Statistic	3.297
Panel ρ -Statistic	–6.035
Panel t -Statistic (non-parametric)	–5.875
Panel t -Statistic (parametric)	–5.646
Group ρ -Statistic	–4.081
Group t -Statistic (non-parametric)	–5.574
Group t -Statistic (parametric)	–5.626

Note: All reported value are distributed N(0,1) under null of no cointegration.
Panel statistics are weighted by long-run variance.

9.4.3 Panel Cointegration Estimation

Having found that trade balance and the terms of trade have a cointegrating relation, we are now ready to estimate this cointegrating relation and determine whether the ML condition is satisfied. As we stressed before, if the ML condition is satisfied in the long-run, then an increase in the terms of trade can be expected to increase the trade balance, and thus the terms of trade have a positive coefficient.

Table 9.3 shows the empirical results of individual FMOLS (fully modified ordinary least squares) and the group-mean panel FMOLS developed by Pedroni (2001). FMOLS estimates and t-statistics for $H_0 : \beta_i = 0$ against $H_A : \beta_i > 0$ are reported in the table.

The results from both the individual tests and the panel tests reject the null hypothesis. Among the individual country tests, the null hypothesis is rejected for fourteen out of nineteen countries at the 1% level, and fifteen out of nineteen countries at the 10% level. For the panel tests, coefficient of the terms of trade is estimated to be 0.31 and its t-statistic is 16.23. The null hypothesis is rejected at the 1% significance level and the positive coefficient is empirically supported. We can thus conclude that the ML condition is empirically supported in sub-Saharan African countries. That is, an increase in the terms of trade increases the trade balance in the long-run.

Table 9.3. Results of panel FMOLS

Country	Coefficient of the Terms of Trade	t -stat
Individual FMOLS Results		
Benin	–0.02	–0.08
Burkina Faso	–0.01	–0.50
Cameroon	0.42	6.06**
Chad	0.53	2.99**
Congo, Rep	0.58	4.42**
Côte d'Ivoire	0.26	5.44**
Gabon	0.47	5.23**
Ghana	0.02	1.28
Guinea-Bissau	0.27	5.04**
Kenya	0.20	7.17**
Madagascar	0.18	4.44**
Malawi	0.89	5.55**
Mali	0.42	4.50**
Nigeria	0.47	5.84**
Rwanda	0.16	3.58**
Senegal	0.18	2.85**
South Africa	0.02	0.23
Togo	0.13	1.49*
Zambia	0.62	5.24**
Panel Group FMOLS Results	0.31	16.23**

Note:
t -stats are for $H_0 : \beta_i = 0.0$.
* and ** indicate 10% and 1% rejection levels, respectively.

9.5 Conclusion

This chapter has applied the recent development of non-stationary panel data analysis to examine the long-run relationship between the trade balance and the terms of trade for 19 sub-Saharan African countries. Using the methodologies of Haynes and Stone (1982) and Arize (1996), we directly analyze the long-run relationship between the two variables. This is an attractive and practical approach which requires no estimations of the import and export demand function.

The results of the panel unit root tests suggest that all of the series considered in the study are nonstationary integrated variables. The major finding, based on Pedroni (1999)'s panel cointegration test, suggests that the trade balance and the terms of trade are cointegrated. Moreover, we can obtain a significant positive estimate for the coefficient of the terms of trade with the use of the group-mean panel FMOLS developed by Pedroni (2001). This implies that the Marshall-Lerner condition is satisfied in the long run, and accordingly, that deterioration in the terms of trade will improve a country's trade balance.

References

Arize, A. (1990) An econometric investigation of export behavior in seven Asian developing countries, *Applied Economic*, **22,** 891-904.

Arize, A. (1996) Cointegration test of a long-run relation between the trade balance and the terms of trade in sixteen countries, *North American Journal of Economics and Finance*, **7**, 203-215.

Baltagi, B.H. (2005) *Econometric Analysis of Panel Data*, 3rd edn, John Wiley & Sons, Chichester.

Breitung, J. (2000) The local power of some unit root tests for panel data, *Advances in Econometrics*, **15**, 161-177.

Goldstein, M. and Khan, M.S. (1978) The supply and demand for exports: A simultaneous approach, *Review of Economics and Statistics*, **60**, 275-286.

Granger, C.W.J. and Newbold, P. (1974) Spurious regression in econometrics, *Journal of Econometrics*, **2**, 111-120.

Haynes, S.E. and Stone, J.A. (1982) Impact of the terms of trade on the U.S. trade balance: A reexamination, *Review of Economics and Statistics*, **64**, 702-706.

Houthakker, H.S. and Magee, S.P. (1969) Income and price elasticities in world trade, *Review of Economics and Statistics*, **51**, 111-125.

Levin, A., Lin, C.F. and Chu, C. (2002) Unit root tests in panel data: Asymptotic and finite-sample properties, *Journal of Econometrics*, **108**, 1-24.

Newey, W. and West, K. (1987) A simple positive semi-definite, heteroscedasticity and autocorrelation consistent covariance matrix, *Econometrica*, **50**, 703-708.

Pedroni, P. (1999) Critical values for cointegration tests in heterogeneous panels with multiple regressors, *Oxford Bulletin of Economics and Statistics*, **61**, 653-670.

Pedroni, P. (2001) Purchasing power parity tests in cointegrated panels, *Review of Economics and Statistics*, **83**, 727-731.,

Phillips, P.C.B. and Moon, H.R. (2000) Nonstationary panel data analysis: an overview of some recent developments, *Econometric Reviews*, **19**, 263-286.

Warner, D. and Kreinin, M. (1983) Determinants of international trade flow, *Review of Economics and Statistics*, **65**, 96-104.

10 Purchasing Power Parity

10.1 Introduction

The theory of purchasing power parity (PPP) came into general use after it was originally formulated by Gustav Cassel in 1922. According to the PPP theory, the long-run equilibrium exchange rate of two currencies is the rate that equalizes the purchasing powers of the currencies. Over the long term, the exchange rate between the currencies adjusts in accordance with the relative purchasing power of each. When the domestic prices of a country increase (inflation), the exchange rate of the country's currency must fall in order to return to PPP. The PPP theory is based on an extension and variation of the law of one price; i.e. that identical goods must have only one price in an efficient market. Thus, in the absence of transportation and other transaction costs, competitive markets will equalize the prices of an identical good in two countries when the prices are expressed in the same currency.[1]

A PPP exchange rate equalizes the purchasing power of different currencies for a given basket of goods (Fig. 10.1). These special exchange rates are often used to compare the standards of living of two or more countries.[2] The OECD (2006), e.g. has provided Purchasing Power Parities (PPPs) for OECD member countries since 1980.

The simplicity and intuitive appeal of PPP has attracted many researchers and prompted many analyses of the theory. A search of the American Economic Association's EconLit, a leading database of economics literature, resulted in 1139 articles (as of September 2006) that have been published since 1969 and use the term "purchasing power parity." Some prominent examples are Enders (1988), Corbae and Ouliaris (1988), Papell (1997), O'Connell (1998) and Pedroni (2001).

---

[1] PPP is often called absolute PPP to distinguish it from a related theory called relative PPP. Relative PPP shows the relationship between the two countries' relative inflation rates and the change in the exchange rate of their currencies.

[2] The simple approach to calculate purchasing power parity between two countries is to compare the price of an identical good across countries. The Economist magazine publishes a "Big Mac Index," which compares the price of a hamburger (Big Mac) around the world (http://www.economist.com/markets/Bigmac/Index.cfm).

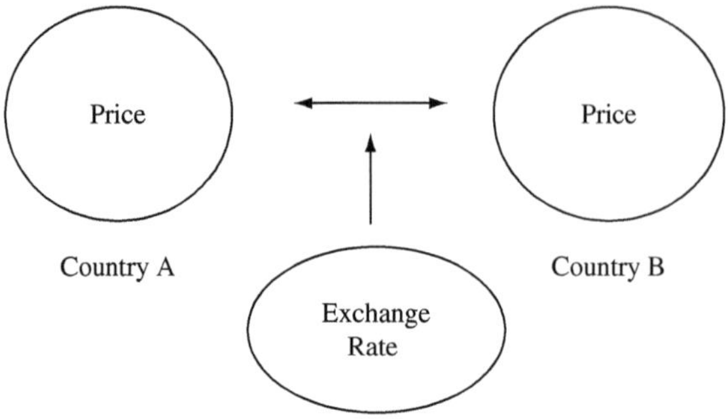

Fig. 10.1. Purchasing power parity

Enders (1988) empirically analyzes the purchasing power parity between the United States and its major trading partners (Canada, Japan and Germany) using ARIMA (auto-regressive integrated moving average) and cointegration techniques. He uses the data for the Bretton Woods and flexible exchange rate periods. Empirical results provide mixed evidence of PPP.

Corbae and Ouliaris (1988) tests whether PPP holds between the United States and some industrialized countries such as Canada, France, Germany, Italy, Japan and the United Kingdom using the theory of cointegration process. Since the null hypothesis of a unit root is not rejected for the real exchange rate, they claim that the long-run absolute version of PPP is rejected.

Papell (1997) empirically investigates the long-run PPP using panel data methods. He tests for unit roots in real exchange rates between the United States and 20 industrialized countries under the current float system. Empirical results as a whole are found to be consistent with long-run PPP.

O'Connell (1998) points out the importance of controlling for cross-sectional dependence when testing for a unit root in panels of real exchange rates. Controlling for cross-sectional dependence, he finds no evidence against the random walk in panels of up to 64 real exchange rates. He also suggests that cross-sectional heterogeneity might be important to reconcile with the time series evidence that has been found in favor of PPP.

Pedroni (2001), among others, developed a technique to test hypotheses in cointegrated panels for the testing of purchasing power parity. To its great advantage, this technique pools only information concerning the long-run hypothesis of interest and allows the short-run dynamics to be potentially heterogeneous. Through this approach, we no longer need to construct estimators that force us to apply similar transmission dynamics among the different countries of the panel. Using monthly data on 20 countries from June 1973 to November 1993, Pedroni (2001) reports the rejection of the PPP hypothesis.[3]

This chapter expands on this Pedroni (2001) analysis by empirically analyzing the PPP hypothesis in the countries of sub-Saharan Africa. Through this approach, we can explicitly consider the heterogeneous characteristics of each country of sub-Saharan Africa.

10.2 Basic Model

According to the theory of purchasing power parity, the exchange rate between one currency and another is in equilibrium when the domestic purchasing powers of the currencies at that rate of exchange are equivalent. In other words, the exchange rate adjusts so that an identical good in two different countries has the same price when expressed in the same currency. Because of its simplicity and intuitive appeal, PPP has been used extensively in theoretical models of exchange rate determination.

PPP can be written as follows:

$$k\frac{S_t P_t^*}{P_t} = 1, \tag{10.1}$$

where k is a constant, S_t is exchange rates at time t, P_t^* is the foreign price level at time t, and P_t is the price level at time t. Taking the logarithms of (10.1) and rearranging the equation, we get,

$$s_t = \alpha + rp_t, \tag{10.2}$$

where $s_t = \log(S_t)$, $\alpha = -\log(k)$, and $rp_t = \log(P_t/P_t^*)$. Based on (10.2), we use the empirical specification as follows:

$$s_t = \alpha + \beta rp_t + u_t, \tag{10.3}$$

where β is a constant and u_t is a stochastic disturbance.

If two conditions are satisfied in this case,

(1) exchange rates (s_t) and CPI ratios (rp_t) are cointegrated, and

(2) $\beta = 1$,

then we can conclude that the strong PPP holds.

[3] Basher and Mohsin (2004) apply the empirical techniques developed by Pedroni (2001) to a set of Asian developing countries and report the rejection of PPP.

10.3 Data

This chapter analyzes 28 sub-Saharan African countries using annual data for the period between 1980 and 2004: Botswana; Burkina Faso; Burundi; Cameroon; Cape Verde; Central African Republic; Democratic Republic of the Congo; Côte d'Ivoire; Gambia; Ghana; Kenya; Lesotho; Madagascar; Malawi; Mauritius; Niger; Nigeria; Rwanda; Senegal; Seychelles; Sierra Leone; South Africa; Sudan; Swaziland; Tanzania; Togo; Uganda; Zimbabwe.

The data were obtained from the World Development Indicators (The World Bank). Bilateral US dollar exchange rates and aggregate consumer price (CPI) index ratios are employed for empirical analysis. Both variables are measured in logarithms. The aggregate CPI index ratios of the sub-Saharan African countries are ratios to the aggregate CPI index of the US.

Figures 10.2 through 10.29 show the movements of the log of exchange rates (s_t) and the log of CPI index ratios (rp_t) for each country. The data suggest that the nominal exchange rates and CPI ratios move together in many of the countries. Thus, there may be a cointegrating relation between the two variables in many of the countries.

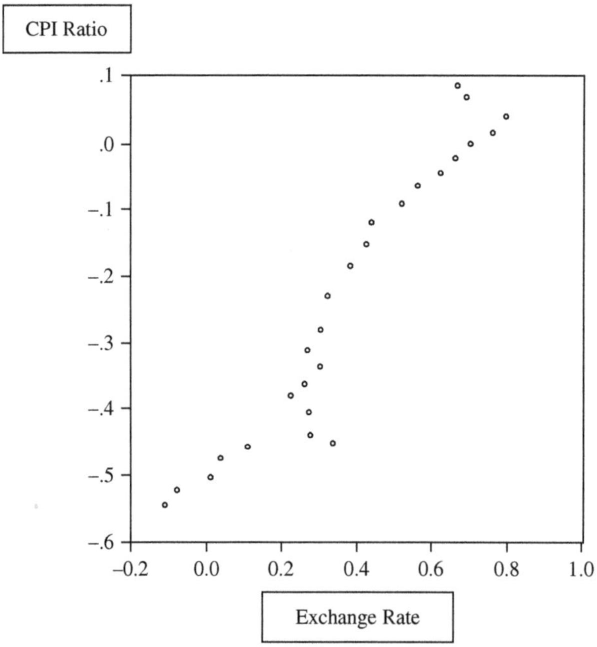

Fig. 10.2. Exchange rate and CPI ratio: Botswana

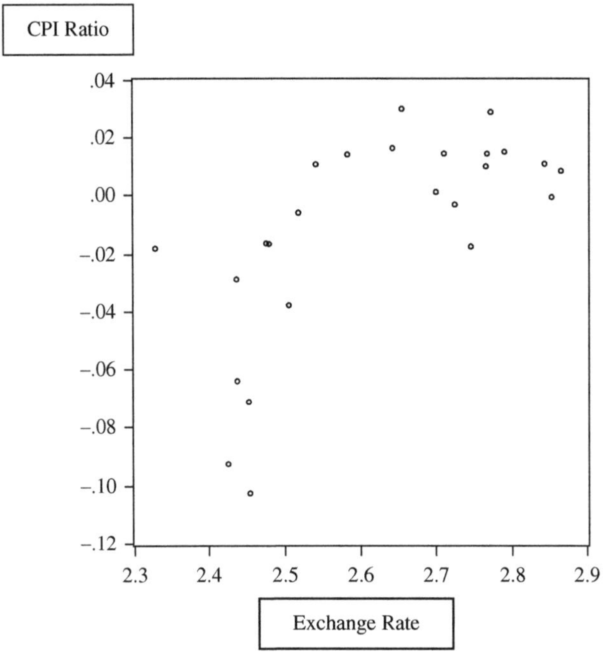

Fig. 10.3. Exchange rate and CPI ratio: Burkina Faso

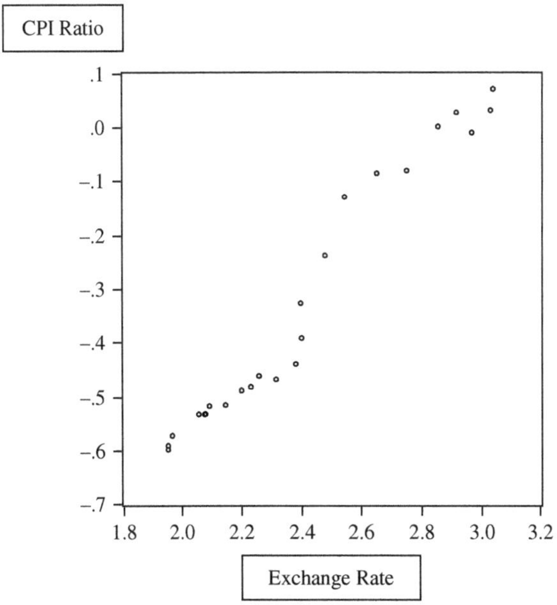

Fig. 10.4. Exchange rate and CPI ratio: Burundi

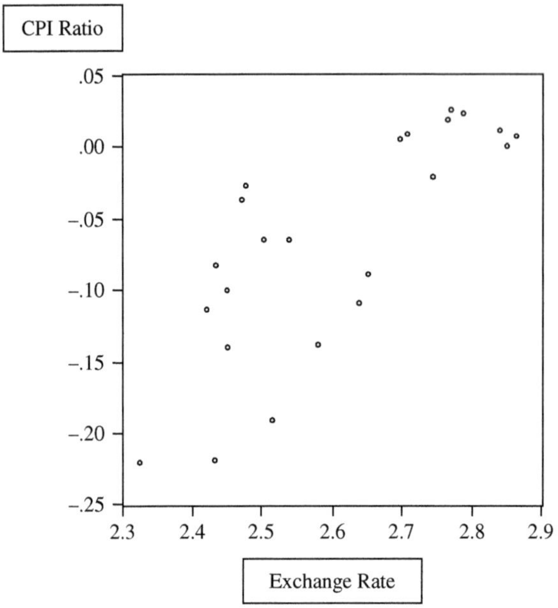

Fig. 10.5. Exchange rate and CPI ratio: Cameroon

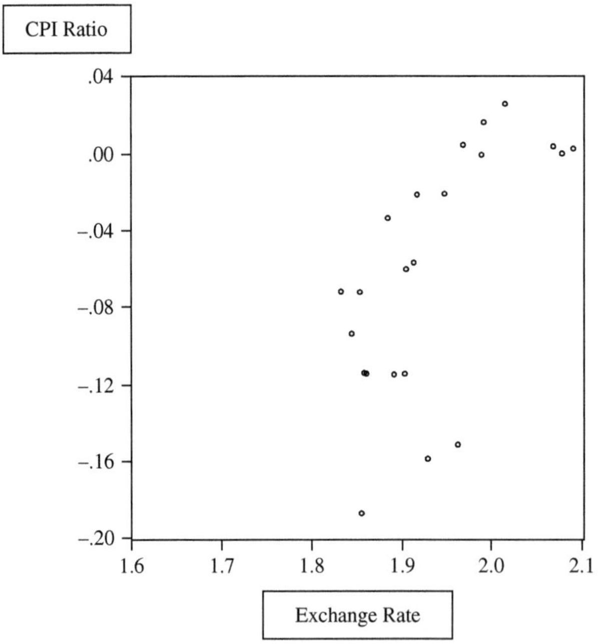

Fig. 10.6. Exchange rate and CPI ratio: Cape Verde

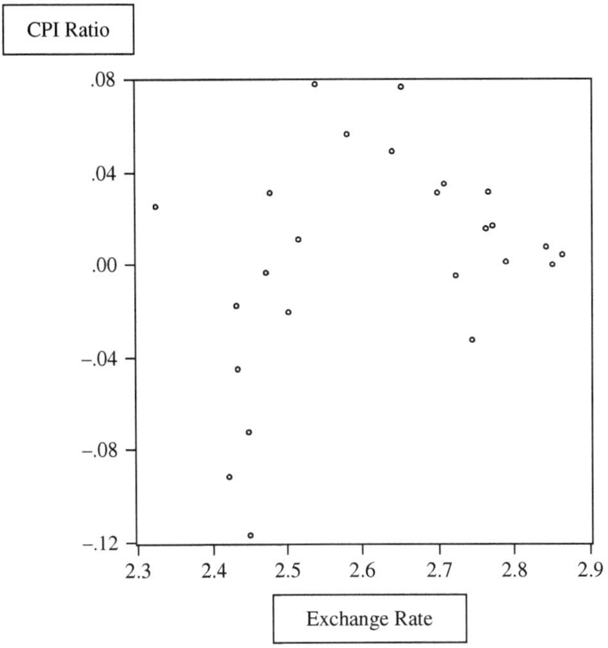

Fig. 10.7. Exchange rate and CPI ratio: Central African Republic

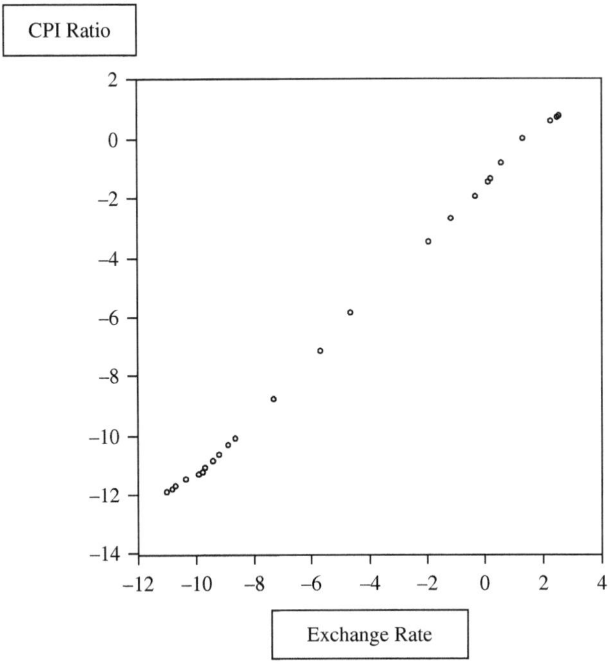

Fig. 10.8. Exchange rate and CPI ratio: Democratic Republic of the Congo

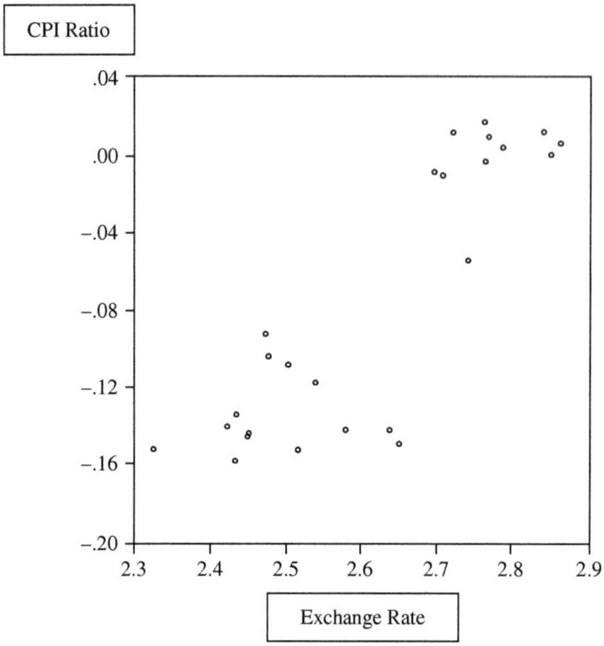

Fig. 10.9. Exchange rate and CPI ratio: Côte d'Ivoire

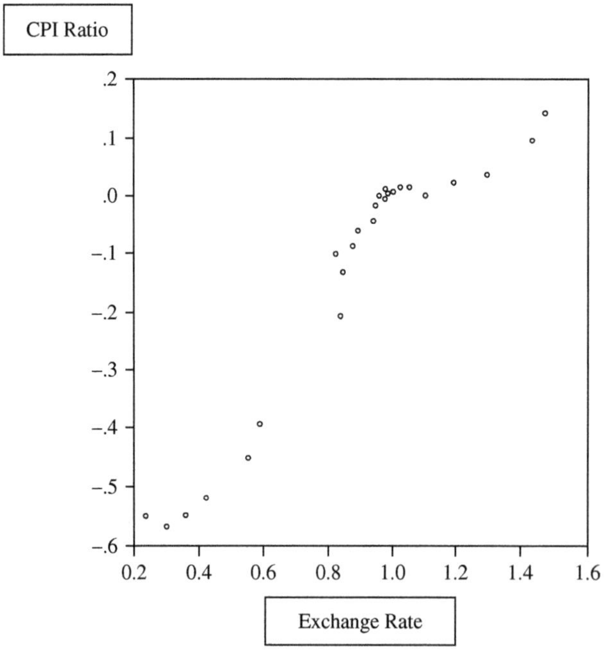

Fig. 10.10. Exchange rate and CPI ratio: Gambia

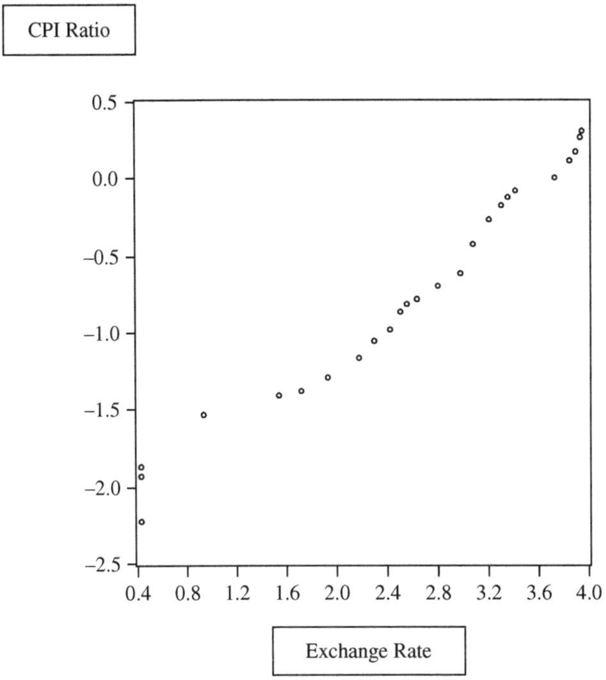

Fig. 10.11. Exchange rate and CPI ratio: Ghana

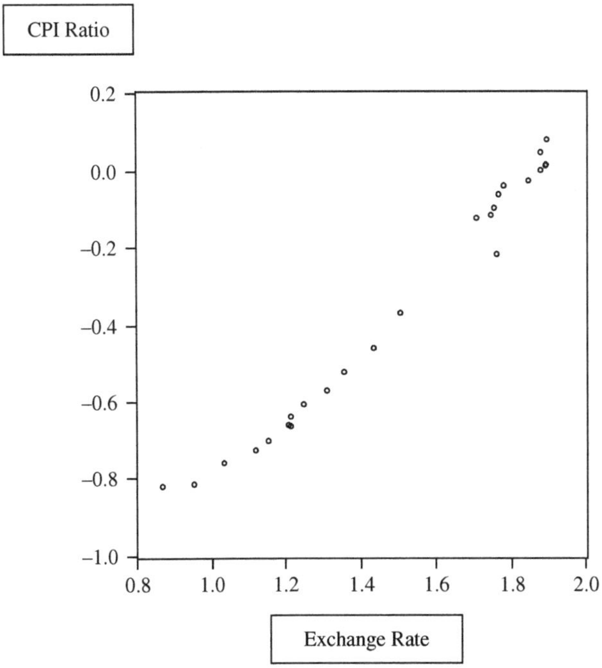

Fig. 10.12. Exchange rate and CPI ratio: Kenya

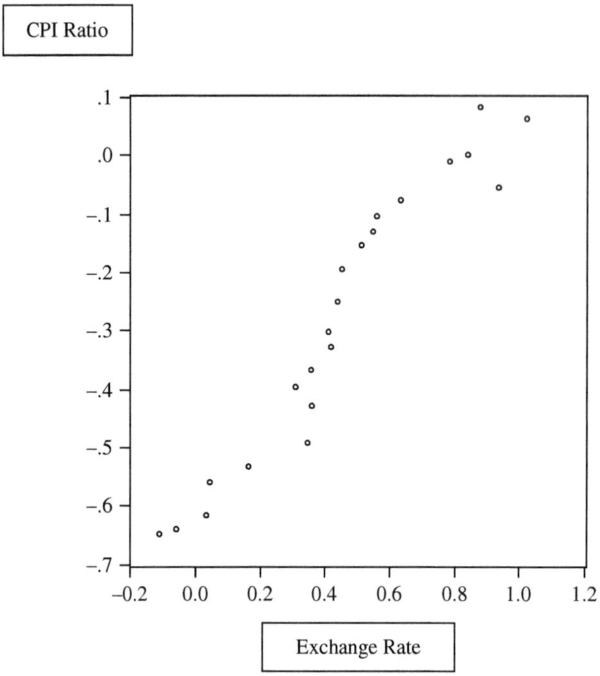

Fig. 10.13. Exchange rate and CPI ratio: Lesotho

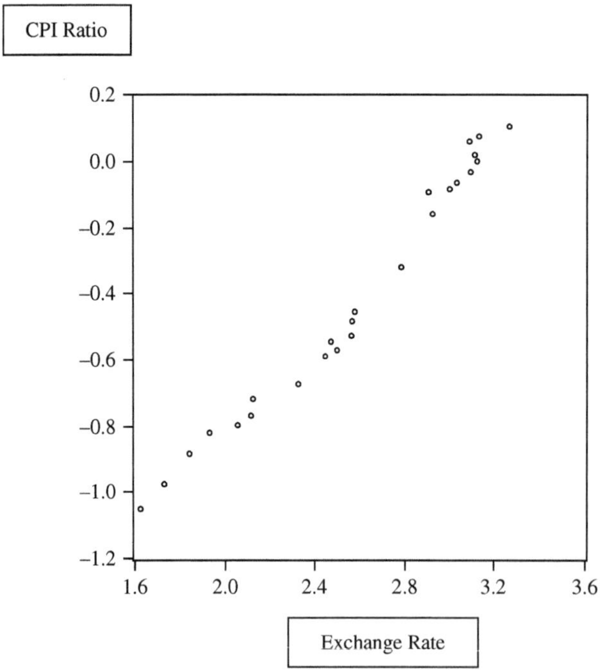

Fig. 10.14. Exchange rate and CPI ratio: Madagascar

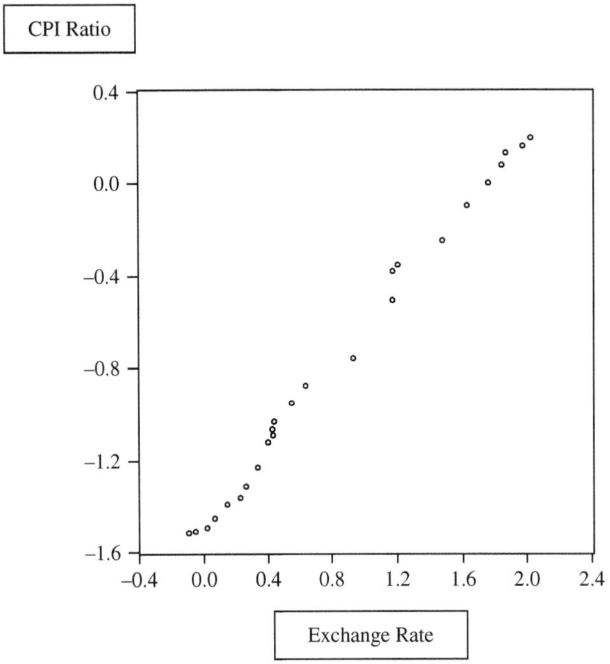

Fig. 10.15. Exchange rate and CPI ratio: Malawi

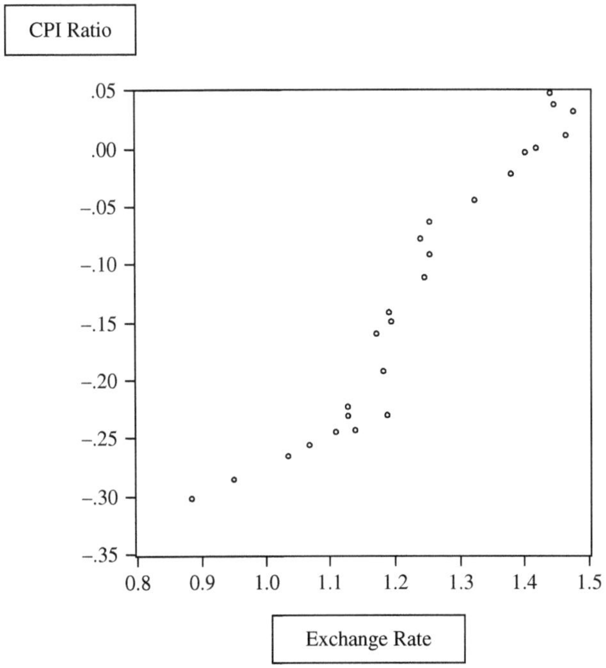

Fig. 10.16. Exchange rate and CPI ratio: Mauritius

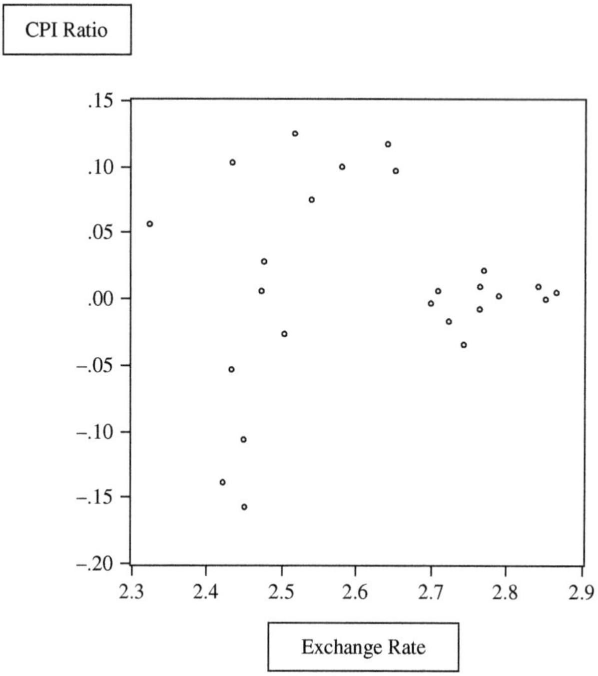

Fig. 10.17. Exchange rate and CPI ratio: Niger

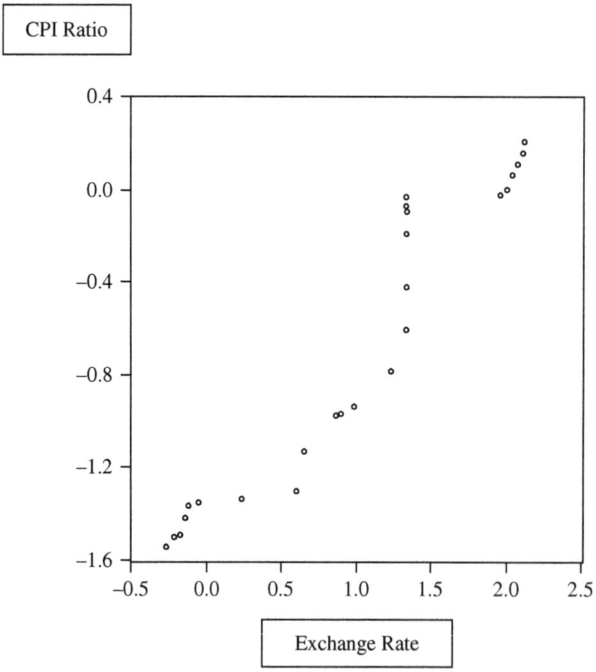

Fig. 10.18. Exchange rate and CPI Ratio: Nigeria

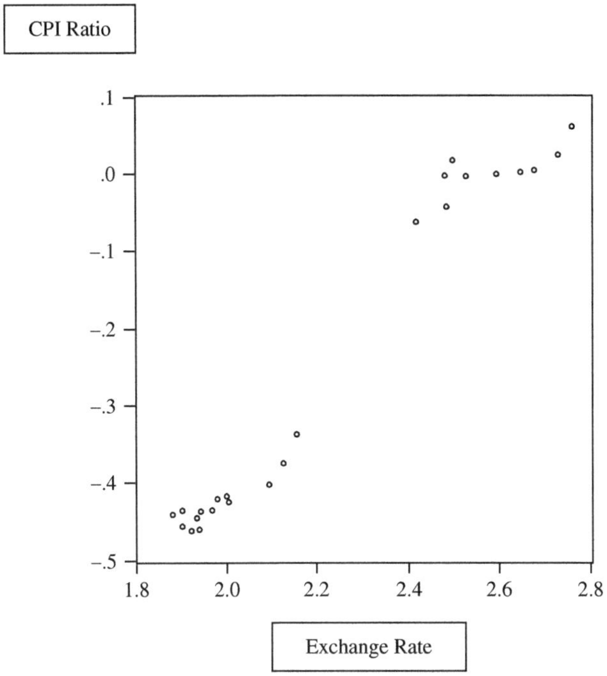

Fig. 10.19. Exchange rate and CPI ratio: Rwanda

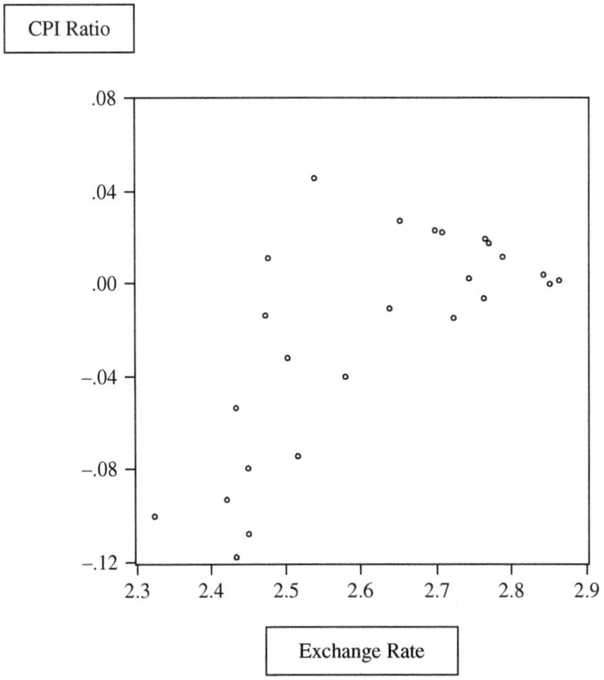

Fig. 10.20. Exchange rate and CPI ratio: Senegal

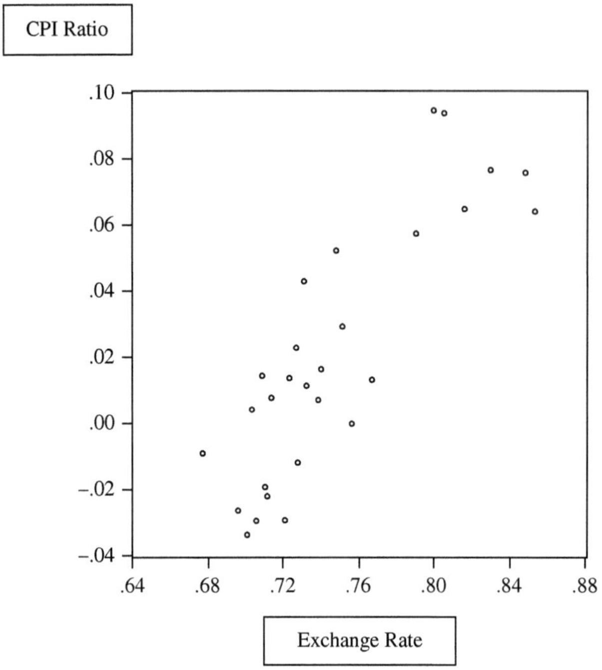

Fig. 10.21. Exchange rate and CPI ratio: Seychelles

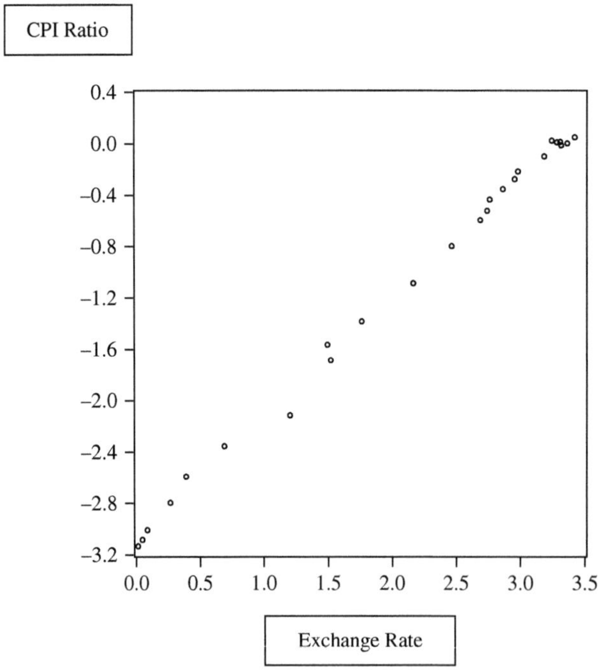

Fig. 10.22. Exchange rate and CPI ratio: Sierra Leone

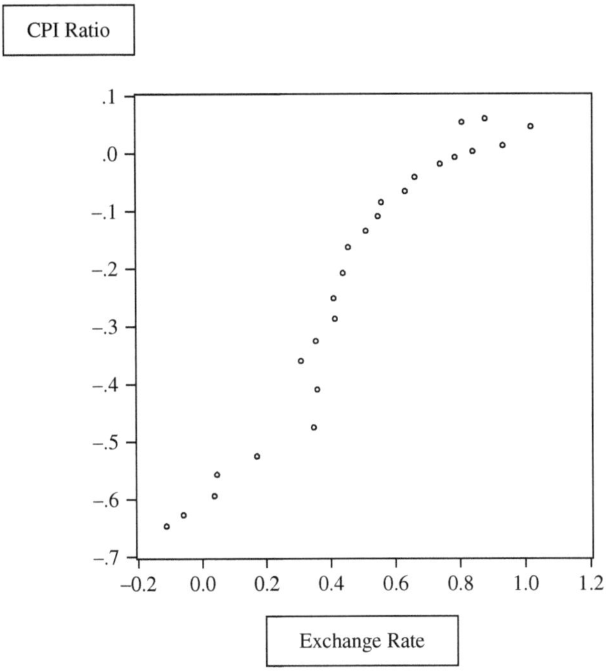

Fig. 10.23. Exchange rate and CPI ratio: South Africa

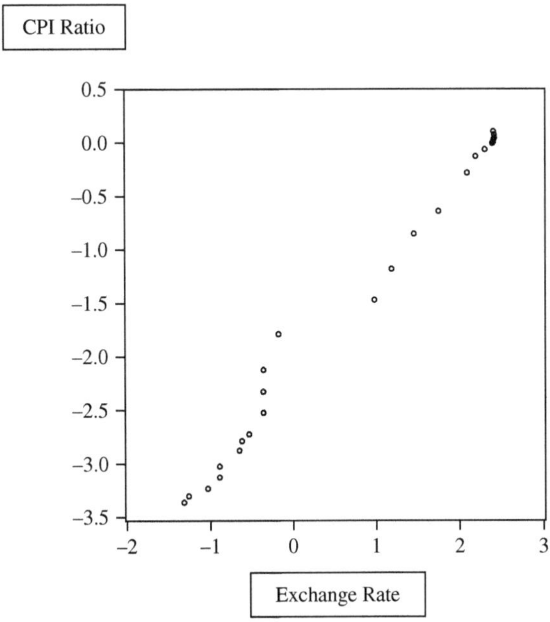

Fig. 10.24. Exchange rate and CPI ratio: Sudan

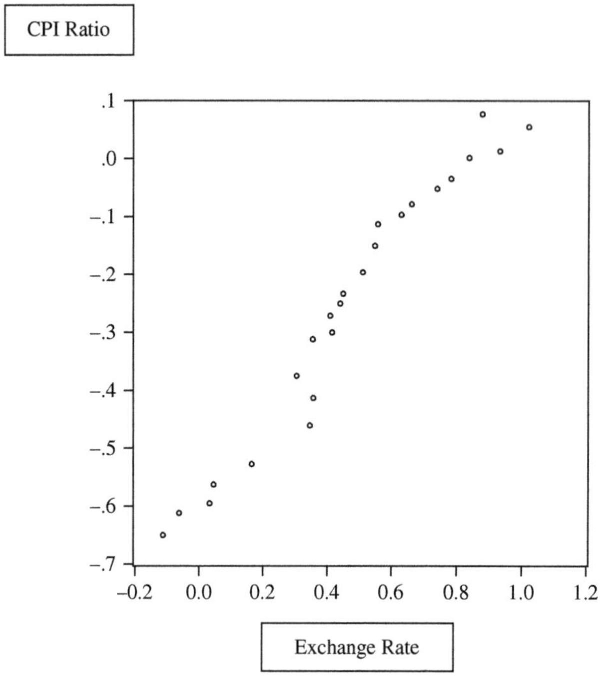

Fig. 10.25. Exchange rate and CPI ratio: Swaziland

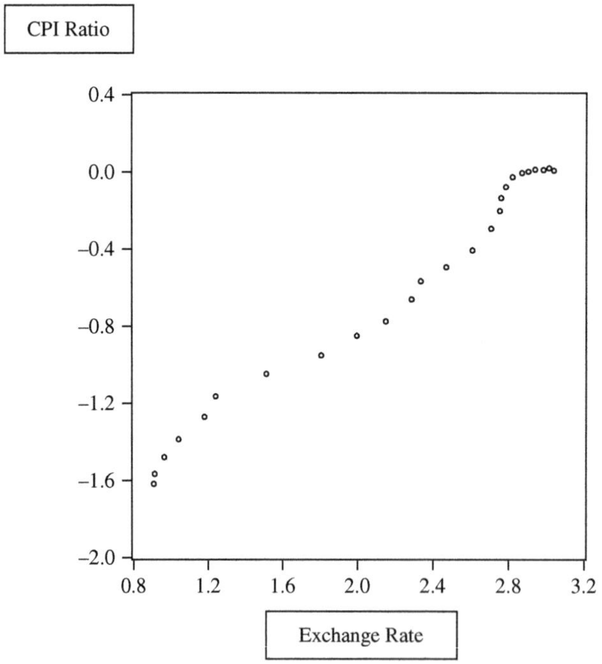

Fig. 10.26. Exchange rate and CPI ratio: Tanzania

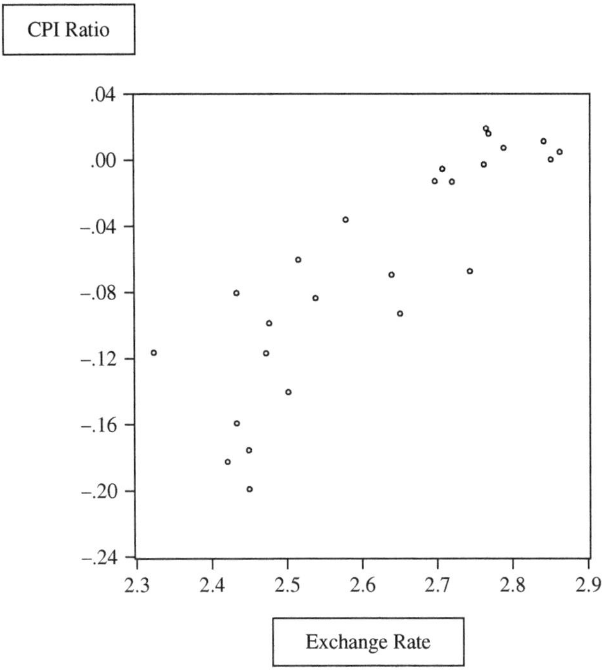

Fig. 10.27. Exchange rate and CPI ratio: Togo

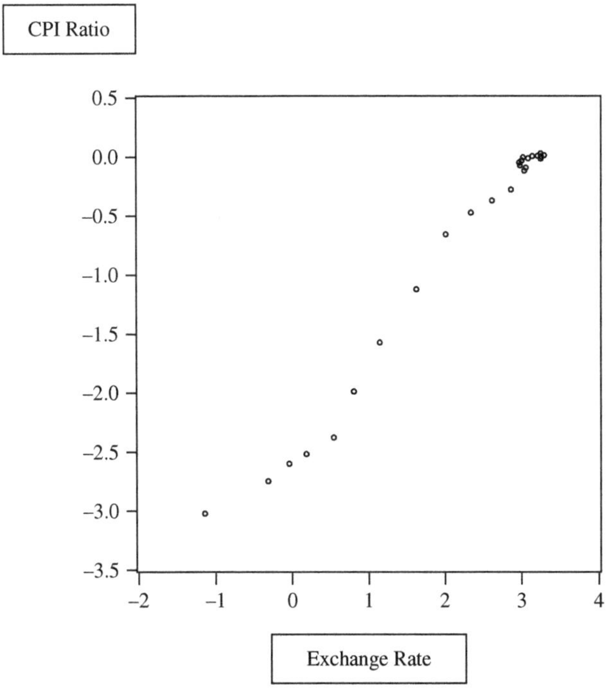

Fig. 10.28. Exchange rate and CPI ratio: Uganda

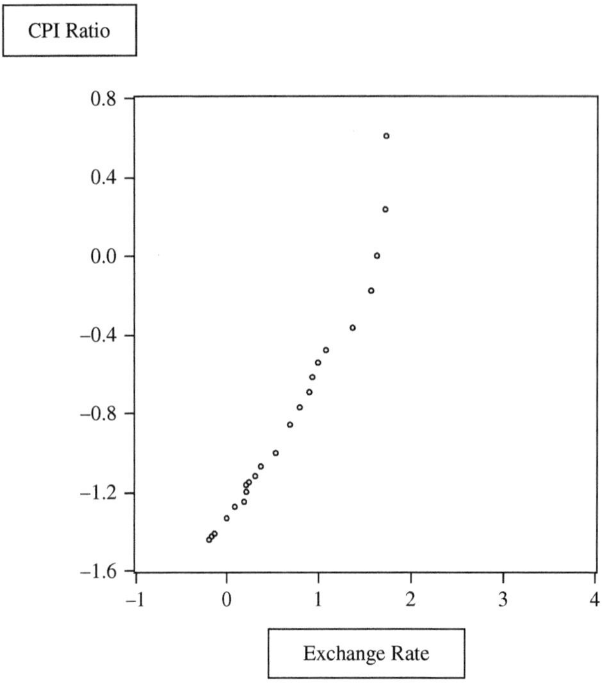

Fig. 10.29. Exchange rate and CPI ratio: Zimbabwe

10.4 Empirical Analysis

10.4.1 Panel Unit Root Tests

To begin with, we need to perform unit root tests on exchange rates and relative CPI ratios. In doing so, however, the use of annual data in this study forces us to work with fairly small sample sizes for each country. Levin et al. (2002) suggest that individual unit root tests have limited power against alternative hypotheses, especially in small samples. Panel unit root tests help us to overcome the problem.[4]

We use three types of panel unit root tests for empirical analysis. One is the IPS test proposed by Im et al. (2003) and the other is the Fisher-type tests developed by Maddala and Wu (1999) and Choi (2001). Both IPS and Fisher-type tests combine information based on individual unit root tests.

[4] Phillips and Moon (2000) and Baltagi (2005, Chap. 12) are good reference for nonstationary panel data analysis.

These tests have the advantage over LLC test (Levin et al., 2002) in that they do not require the homogeneous autoregressive coefficients under the alternative hypothesis.

For IPS and Fisher-type tests, we use the following ADF regression for each cross section:

$$\Delta y_{i,t} = \alpha y_{i,t-1} + \sum_{j=1}^{p_i} \beta_{i,j} \Delta y_{i,t-j} + \delta_{0,i} + \delta_{1,i} t + \varepsilon_{i,t} \ , \tag{10.4}$$

where $i = 1, 2, \cdots, N$ are the cross-section series observed over periods $t = 1, 2, \cdots T_i$; $\delta_{0,i}$ are fixed effects, $\delta_{1,i} t$ are individual time trends; Δ is the difference operator, i.e. $\Delta y_{i,t} = y_{i,t} - y_{i,t-1}$; and the errors ε_{it} are assumed to be mutually independent disturbances.

The null hypothesis is expressed as,

$$H_0 : \alpha_i = 0, \text{ for all } i,$$

while the alternative hypothesis is given by:

$$H_A : \begin{cases} \alpha_i = 0, & \text{for } i = 1, 2, \cdots, N_1, \\ \alpha_i < 0, & \text{for } i = N_1 + 1, N_1 + 2, \cdots, N. \end{cases}$$

The null hypothesis is that each series in the panel has a unit root and the alternative hypothesis allows for some (but not all) of the individual series to have unit roots.

The IPS t-bar statistic is defined as the average of the individual ADF statistics as follows:

$$\bar{t} = \frac{1}{N} \sum_{i=1}^{N} t_i \ , \tag{10.5}$$

where t_i is the individual t-statistics for α_i in (10.4). Then, Im et al. (2003) show that a properly standardized t-bar statistic has an asymptotic standardized normal distribution:

$$W = \frac{\sqrt{N}\left(\bar{t} - \frac{1}{N}\sum_{i=1}^{N} E[t_i]\right)}{\sqrt{\frac{1}{N}\sum_{i=1}^{N} V[t_i]}} \to N(0,1), \tag{10.6}$$

where the value of $E[t_i]$ and $V[t_i]$ are provided by Im et al. (2003) via simulations.

Alternatively, Maddala and Wu (1999) and Choi (2001) proposed a Fisher-type test (Fisher, 1932) that combines the p-values from individual unit root tests. Let p_i be the p-value from unit root tests for each cross-section i to test for unit root in panel data, then Maddala and Wu (1999) show that

$$-2\sum_{i=1}^{N} \ln(p_i) \rightarrow \chi^2(2N). \tag{10.7}$$

Choi (2001) also shows that

$$Z = \frac{1}{\sqrt{N}}\sum_{i=1}^{N} \Phi^{-1}(p_i) \rightarrow N(0,1), \tag{10.8}$$

where Φ^{-1} is the inverse of the standard normal cumulative distribution function.

Table 10.1 shows the results of panel unit root tests performed on exchange rates. The IPS test statistics, the Fisher-type test statistics and their respective p-values are included. The AIC was used as the criterion for selecting the number of lags in the ADF regression for cross sections, (10.4). Individual constant and individual trends are included for the deterministic component.

From the results in Table 10.1, we find that the IPS test statistic and its p-value are 1.449 and 0.926 for the level of exchange rates, and -8.960 and 0.000 for the first difference of exchange rates. We obtain the similar results when we use Fisher-type tests. Thus, the exchange rate has a unit root.

Table 10.1. Results of panel unit root test: exchange rate

	Method	Test Statistics	p-value
Level	IPS	1.449	0.926
	Fisher Chi-square	44.017	0.877
	Fisher Z-stat	1.584	0.943
First Difference	IPS	–8.960	0.000
	Fisher Chi-square	183.562	0.000
	Fisher Z-stat	–8.5472	0.000

Note:
The null hypothesis is no unit root.
IPS is the Im, Pesaran and Shin (2003) test.
Fisher Chi-square is the Maddala and Wu (1999) test.
Fisher Z-stat is the Choi test (2001).
p-value for the Fisher Chi-square test is computed using an asymptotic chi-square distribution. All other tests assume asymptotic normality.

Table 10.2. Results of panel unit root test: CPI ratio

	Method	Test Statistics	p-value
Level	IPS	1.583	0.943
	Fisher Chi-square	54.593	0.528
	Fisher Z-stat	2.044	0.980
First Difference	IPS	–6.228	0.000
	Fisher Chi-square	141.692	0.000
	Fisher Z-stat	–5.831	0.000

Note:
The null hypothesis is no unit root.
IPS is the Im, Pesaran and Shin (2003) test.
Fisher Chi-square is the Maddala and Wu (1999) test.
Fisher Z-stat is the Choi test (2001).
p-value for the Fisher Chi-square test is computed using an asymptotic chi-square distribution. All other tests assume asymptotic normality.

Table 10.2 shows the results of panel unit root tests performed on the CPI ratio. The results indicate that the IPS test statistic and its p-value are 1.583 and 0.943 for the level of the CPI ratio, and -6.228 and 0.000 for the first difference of the CPI ratio. Here too, we obtain the similar results for Fisher-type tests. Thus, the CPI ratio has a unit root as well.

Thus, we can say that the exchange rates and CPI ratios are non-stationary variables with a unit root.

10.4.2 Panel Cointegration Tests

The two series were unable to reject the null of the unit root. Our next step, therefore, is to perform the cointegration test. We begin by implementing the following equation:

$$s_{i,t} = \alpha_i + \beta_i rp_{i,t} + u_{i,t}, \quad i = 1, 2, \cdots, N;\ t = 1, 2, \cdots, T, \qquad (10.3')$$

where $s_{i,t}$ is the log of bilateral US nominal exchange rate, $rp_{i,t}$ is the log of aggregate price ratio in terms of the CPI between the two countries, α_i and β_i are constant for country i, and $u_{i,t}$ is the disturbance term for a country i at time t.

In a bivariate context, Pedroni (1999) develops asymptotic and finite-sample properties of the test statistic to test the null hypothesis of no-cointegration in the panel. While both the homogeneous and heterogeneous panel models are possible, the heterogeneous model such as (10.3') is consistent with the class of model when parameters α and β are allowed to vary across countries. Having no reason to believe that all of the parameters are the same across countries, as is assumed in the homogeneous model, we employ the heterogeneous model in our analysis.

Pedroni (1999) derives the asymptotic distribution and explores the small sample performances of seven different statistics. Of these seven statistics, four are based on pooling along what is commonly referred to as the "within-dimension" and three are based on pooling along what is commonly referred to as the "between-dimension." Pedroni (1999) describes the former and latter as "panel cointegration statistics" and "group mean panel cointegration statistics."

The first of the simple panel cointegration statistics, the "panel ν-statistic", is a non-parametric variance ratio statistic. The second, the "panel ρ-statistic", is a panel version of a non-parametric statistic analogous to the familiar Phillips and Perron ρ-statistic. The third, the "panel t-statistic (non-parametric)", is a non-parametric statistic analogous to the Phillips and Perron t-statistic. The fourth of these simple panel cointegration statistics, the "panel t – statistic (parametric)", is a parametric statistic analogous to the familiar augmented Dickey-Fuller t-statistic.[5]

The other three panel cointegration statistics are based on a group mean approach. The first, the "group ρ-statistic", is analogous to the Phillips and Perron ρ-statistic. The last two, the "group t-statistic (non-parametric)" and the "group t-statistic (parametric)", are analogous to the Phillips and Perron t-statistic and the augmented Dickey-Fuller t-statistic, respectively.

Table 10.3 shows the results of panel cointegration tests performed on exchange rates and CPI ratios. The test statistics are as follows: 2.898 for the panel ν-statistic, -2.358 for the panel ρ-statistic, -3.207 for the non-parametric panel t-statistic, -4.014 for parametric the panel t-statistic, -0.306 for the group ρ-statistic, -2.458 for the non-parametric group t-statistic, and -4.633 for the parametric group t-statistic. This table clearly indicates that the null hypothesis of no cointegration is rejected for most cases. Thus, exchange rates and CPI ratios are cointegrated in the countries of sub-Saharan Africa.

[5] See Table 1 of Pedroni (1999, p.660).

Table 10.3. Results of panel cointegration test

Method	Test Statistic
Panel ν -Statistic	2.898
Panel ρ -Statistic	–2.358
Panel t -Statistic (non-parametric)	–3.207
Panel t -Statistic (parametric)	–4.014
Group ρ -Statistic	–0.306
Group t -Statistic (non-parametric)	–2.458
Group t -Statistic (parametric)	–4.633

Note: All reported value are distributed N(0,1) under null of no cointegration.
Panel statistics are weighted by long-run variance.

10.4.3 Panel Cointegration Estimation

Having found that exchange rates and CPI ratios have a cointegrating relation, we are now ready to estimate this cointegrating relation and examine whether the strong PPP is satisfied.

Table 10.4 shows the empirical results of individual FMOLS (fully modified ordinary least squares) and the group-mean panel FMOLS developed by Pedroni (2001). The table gives the FMOLS estimates and t -statistics for $H_0 : \beta_i = 1$ against $H_A : \beta_i \neq 1$. The results from both the individual tests and the panel tests reject the null hypothesis. For the individual country tests, data from 21 out of 28 countries produce rejections at the 10% level. For the panel test, the coefficient of CPI ratio is estimated to be 1.36 and t -statistic is 14.77. The reported results clearly reject the null hypothesis at the 1% significance level. We can thus conclude that strong PPP is empirically rejected in the countries of sub-Saharan Africa.

Pedroni (2001) reports that the PPP does not hold true for 20 countries for post Bretton Woods period. Basher and Mohsin (2004) also show that the PPP does not hold for ten Asian developing countries over the period from 1980 to 1999. Our results are consistent with Pedroni (2001) and Basher and Mohsin (2004).

Table 10.4. Results of panel FMOLS

Country	Coefficient of CPI Ratio	t -stat
Individual FMOLS Results		
Botswana	1.20	2.16*
Burkina Faso	3.02	1.91*
Burundi	1.56	5.48**
Cameroon	1.82	1.67
Cape Verde	0.60	−1.22
Central African Republic	1.00	0.00
Congo, Dem. Rep.	1.03	3.62**
Côte d'Ivoire	1.92	2.98**
Gambia	1.39	2.29*
Ghana	1.43	4.39**
Kenya	1.02	0.62
Lesotho	1.26	2.16*
Madagascar	1.31	4.27**
Malawi	1.18	7.13**
Mauritius	1.28	2.77**
Niger	0.04	−1.30
Nigeria	1.23	1.76*
Rwanda	1.43	4.77**
Senegal	2.63	1.80*
Seychelles	1.30	1.33
Sierra Leone	1.07	5.84**
South Africa	1.24	1.95*
Sudan	1.08	2.53*
Swaziland	1.37	4.09**
Tanzania	1.38	5.29**
Togo	2.11	3.85**
Uganda	1.18	4.74**
Zimbabwe	1.09	1.27
Panel Group FMOLS Results	1.36	14.77**

Note:
t -stats are for $H_0 : \beta_i = 1.0$.
* and ** indicate 10% and 1% rejection levels, respectively.

10.5 Conclusion

This chapter has applied the recent development of non-stationary panel data analysis to examine the long-run relationship implied by the purchasing power parity hypothesis for 28 countries of sub-Saharan Africa. Using the methodologies of Pedroni (2001), we empirically analyze the long-run relationship between exchange rates and CPI ratios. Through this attractive and practical approach, we are no longer forced to apply constrained transmission dynamics which are similar among the countries of the panel.

The results of the panel unit root tests suggest that all of the series considered in the study are nonstationary integrated variables. The major finding, based on Pedroni (1999)'s panel cointegration test, suggests that the exchange rates and CPI ratios are cointegrated. With the use of the group-mean panel FMOLS developed by Pedroni (2001), however, we strongly reject the null hypothesis that the coefficient of CPI ratios is one. Though the nominal exchange rate and CPI ratios move together over the long-run, this result implies that the PPP itself does not hold true for the countries of sub-Saharan Africa. The findings from this study are consistent with those of Pedroni (2001) and Basher and Mohsin (2004).

References

Baltagi, B.H. (2005) *Econometric Analysis of Panel Data*, 3rd edn. John Wiley & Sons, Chichester.

Basher, S. and Mohsin, M. (2004) PPP tests in cointegrated panels: evidence from Asian developing countries, *Applied Economics Letters*, **11**, 163-166.

Cassel, G. (1922) *Money and Foreign Exchange after 1914*, Constable and Co, London.

Choi, I. (2001) Unit root tests for panel data, *Journal of International Money and Finance*, **20**, 249-272.

Corbae D. and Ouliaris, S. (1988) Cointegration and tests of purchasing power parity, *Review of Economics and Statistics*, **70**, 508-511.

Enders, W. (1988) ARIMA and cointegrating tests of PPP under fixed and flexible exchange rate regimes, *Review of Economics and Statistics*, **70**, 504-508.

Fisher, R.A. (1932) *Statistical Methods for Research Workers*, 4th edn. Oliver & Boyd, Edinburgh.

Im, K.S., Pesaran, M.H. and Shin, Y. (2003) Testing for unit roots in heterogeneous panels, *Journal of Econometrics*, **115**, 53-74.

Levin, A., Lin, C.F. and Chu, C. (2002) Unit root tests in panel data: Asymptotic and finite-sample properties, *Journal of Econometrics*, **108**, 1-24.

Maddala, G.S. and Wu, S. (1999) A comparative study of unit root tests with panel data and a new simple test, *Oxford Bulletin of Economics and Statistics*, **61**, 631-652.

O'Connell, P.G.J. (1998) The overvaluation of purchasing power parity, *Journal of International Economics*, **44**, 1-19.

OECD. (2006) Purchasing Power Parities, http://www.oecd.org/department/0,2688,en_2649_34357_1_1_1_1_1,00.html.

Papell, D. (1997) Searching for stationarity: purchasing power parity under the current float, *Journal of International Economics*, **43**, 313-332.

Pedroni, P. (1999) Critical values for cointegration tests in heterogeneous panels with multiple regressors, *Oxford Bulletin of Economics and Statistics*, **61**, 653-670.

Pedroni, P. (2001) Purchasing power parity tests in cointegrated panels, *Review of Economics and Statistics*, **83**, 727-731.

Phillips, P.C.B. and Moon, H.R. (2000) Nonstationary panel data analysis: an overview of some recent developments, *Econometric Reviews*, **19**, 263-286.

11 Concluding Remarks

Participation in the globalization process has always been a topic of controversy among researchers and policymakers. The debate tends to be fiercest in discussions on developing countries.

For some developing countries of a certain size or structure, a shift towards complete openness to international trade and investment might bring more disadvantages than benefits. In trade, the relatively low prices and low income elasticities of the products exported by developing countries tend to disallow rapid enhancements. The exports of developing countries also consist largely of primary products which fall in price in world markets and thus bring down the terms of trade. Imports, on the other hand, can drive uncompetitive domestic producers out of business. In the realm of foreign direct investment (FDI), meanwhile, investment mainly targeting a domestic market may "crowd-out" the less competitive domestic firms, while investment committed solely to take advantage of cheap production costs in a host country may fail to fully integrate into the economy or spread potential externality effects.

The professed benefits of international trade are well known. By allowing each country to specialize in its comparative advantage, trade with overseas partners can permit a better or optimal allocation of resources. All participating countries gain. The larger size of the world market allows trade participants to operate at the minimum required levels and to benefit from the increasing return to scale. Competition and exchange with overseas partners also help an economy by pulling up know-how and productivity. Better skill, the various types of knowledge embedded in intermediate goods imported from developed countries improve production processes in developing countries. FDI inflow, meanwhile, can complement or substitute other forms of fresh foreign capital. This is crucial for countries with limited access to international financial markets and diminishing levels of incoming foreign aid. The flow of foreign investments also adds to existing domestic investment, thus providing benefits important for countries with low income and consequently low savings. Finally, FDI acts as a channel for technology transfer from developed to developing countries; indeed, most foreign investment in the latter originates from the former.

Saddled with so many contrasting theories on international trade and FDI, researchers and policymakers spent many years in dispute over the prudence of advocating openness in developing countries. Then, from about the 1980s, the economies which had embraced open policies began to discernibly outperform those which had opted for closed ones. As arguments in favor of participation in international trade and investment gained momentum, the focus of debate shifted to policies for optimizing the benefits of this participation. An important strategy towards this end is to enhance competitiveness in trade and foreign investment.

Our analyses focused on two policies often put in place to strengthen international competitiveness: the exchange rate policy and productivity policy. Our studies mainly focused on the countries of sub-Saharan Africa.

Chapter 2 and Chapter 3 of this book describe our initial investigations on the trade-FDI and growth relationship. These investigations produced three core findings: (i) trade openness and FDI markedly influence growth, (ii) economic growth is more sensitive to trade in sub-Saharan African economies than in the Asian and Latin American economies examined in our analyses, and (iii) the direction of causality runs unilaterally from FDI to economic growth in the sub-Saharan African economies. Thus, a policymaker needs to find measures that can be expected to broaden his or her country's participation in international trade and heighten the inward stock of foreign investments. Key to these measures is their effectiveness in sharpening international competitiveness. The next chapters (Chap. 4 and Chap. 5) focus on the effectiveness of policy measures in bringing about stronger competitiveness in both international trade and foreign direct investment.

In our next investigations on the effectiveness of the exchange rate policy and productivity policy, we found that the former might not be effective in strengthening trade competitiveness. Specifically, our results indicated that the expected falls in export prices due to the devaluation of the currency might be offset by the resulting inflation. Indeed, we established that the depreciation of the local currency pushes up domestic inflation (Chap. 4).

In contrast, higher productivity cuts down the per unit cost of production and allows exportation at lower prices. Indeed, we found a long-run relationship between export prices and productivity in the countries studied more often than a long-run relationship between export prices and the exchange rate (Chap. 5).

Our next investigations explored FDI competitiveness. Specifically, we focused on the determinants of FDI inflow to identify the areas where policymakers can expect to improve a country's attractiveness to foreign investors. The various potential determinants put forward in the literature were also considered. Our two variables of focus, the exchange rate and productivity, were confirmed to be significant determinants of FDI inflow. Both policies can be used to strengthen a host country's appeal to foreign investors. We also found that the higher capital return in sub-Saharan Africa serves as an important incentive for foreign investors in spite of the higher risk (Chap. 6).

Next we investigated the determinants of productivity to identify direct policy measures for increasing productivity. Besides the usual factors such as human capital, infrastructure, and price distortions, we delved into three other factors which have yet to be sufficiently considered in the literature: agglomeration economies, reallocation of production factors, and demographic age structure. Empirical results show that reallocation of production, black market premium, agglomeration economies, and the level of infrastructure development are significant factors to increase productivity (Chap. 7).

Then, through a series of tests on changes in the trade accounts of sub-Saharan African countries, we found that the trade accounts are very likely to be non-stationary variables. Thus, some appropriate policies must be put in place to prevent trade deficits from expanding. This calls for a serious exploration of the available methods for controlling changes in trade accounts (Chap. 8).

Moving forward from the analysis in Chap. 8, we analyzed the long-run relationship between the trade balance and the terms of trade for sub-Saharan African countries. Our findings indicated that the Marshall-Lerner condition is satisfied in the long run, and accordingly, that deterioration in the terms of trade will improve a country's trade balance (Chap. 9).

Finally, we empirically analyzed the long-run relationship implied by the purchasing power parity hypothesis for sub-Saharan Africa. The exchange rates and CPI ratios were found to be cointegrated, but our analysis strongly rejected the null hypothesis that the coefficient of CPI ratios is one. Though the nominal exchange rate and CPI ratios move together over the long-run, this result implies that the PPP itself does not hold true. Thus, the adjustment mechanism of exchange rates has some limitations (Chap. 10).

While the exchange rate might be expected to bring about higher trade and FDI competitiveness, its effectiveness in doing so is rather controversial. Productivity, on the other hand, turns out to be robust in enhancing trade and FDI, and ultimately in improving domestic welfare. The policy measures enumerated above can be used to ameliorate aggregate productivity.

Index

About the Authors

Dr. Ivohasina Fizara Razafimahefa has earned a Ph.D. in Economics from Kobe University, Japan. He has been a Visiting Research Fellow at the Institute of Developing Economies, JETRO, Tokyo, Japan and a Consultant for the United Nations Industrial Development Organization, Vienna, Austria. Currently, he is the Director of Economic Affairs at the Presidency of the Republic of Madagascar.

Professor Shigeyuki Hamori is Professor of Economics at Kobe University in Japan. He earned his PhD in Economics at Duke University. His areas of research are in the field of applied econometrics and he has published widely in numerous journals.

Advanced Studies in Theoretical and Applied Econometrics

1. J.H.P. Paelinck (ed.): *Qualitative and Quantitative Mathematical Economics.* 1982 ISBN 90-247-2623-9
2. J.P. Ancot (ed.): *Analysing the Structure of Econometric Models.* 1984 ISBN 90-247-2894-0
3. A.J. Hughes Hallet (ed.): *Applied Decision Analysis and Economic Behaviour.* 1984 ISBN 90-247-2968-8
4. J.K. Sengupta: *Information and Efficiency in Economic Decision.* 1985 ISBN 90-247-3072-4
5. P. Artus and O. Guvenen (eds.), in collaboration with F. Gagey: *International Macroeconomic Modelling for Policy Decisions.* 1986 ISBN 90-247-3201-8
6. M.J. Vilares: *Structural Change in Macroeconomic Models.* Theory and Estimation. 1986 ISBN 90-247-3277-8
7. C. Carraro and D. Sartore (eds.): *Development of Control Theory for Economic Analysis.* 1987 ISBN 90-247-3345-6
8. D.P. Broer: *Neoclassical Theory and Empirical Models of Aggregate Firm Behaviour.* 1987 ISBN 90-247-3412-6
9. A. Italianer: *Theory and Practice of International Trade Linkage Models.* 1986 ISBN 90-247-3407-X
10. D.A. Kendrick: *Feedback.* A New Framework for Macroeconomic Policy. 1988 ISBN 90-247-3593-9; Pb: 90-247-3650-1
11. J.K. Sengupta and G.K. Kadekodi (eds.): *Econometrics of Planning and Efficiency.* 1988 ISBN 90-247-3602-1
12. D.A. Griffith: *Advanced Spatial Statistics.* Special Topics in the Exploration of Quantitative Spatial Data Series. 1988 ISBN 90-247-3627-7
13. O. Guvenen (ed.): *International Commodity Market Models and Policy Analysis.* 1988 ISBN 90-247-3768-0
14. G. Arbia: *Spatial Data Configuration in Statistical Analysis of Regional Economic and Related Problems.* 1989 ISBN 0-7923-0284-2
15. B. Raj (ed.): *Advances in Econometrics and Modelling.* 1989 ISBN 0-7923-0299-0
16. A. Aznar Grasa: *Econometric Model Selection.* A New Approach. 1989 ISBN 0-7923-0321-0
17. L.R. Klein and J. Marquez (eds.): *Economics in Theory and Practice.* An Eclectic Approach. Essays in Honor of F. G. Adams. 1989 ISBN 0-7923-0410-1
18. D.A. Kendrick: *Models for Analyzing Comparative Advantage.* 1990 ISBN 0-7923-0528-0
19. P. Artus and Y. Barroux (eds.): *Monetary Policy.* A Theoretical and Econometric Approach. 1990 ISBN 0-7923-0626-0
20. G. Duru and J.H.P. Paelinck (eds.): *Econometrics of Health Care.* 1990 ISBN 0-7923-0766-6
21. L. Phlips (ed.): *Commodity, Futures and Financial Markets.* 1991 ISBN 0-7923-1043-8
22. H.M. Amman, D.A. Belsley and L.F. Pau (eds.): *Computational Economics and Econometrics.* 1992 ISBN 0-7923-1287-2
23. B. Raj and J. Koerts (eds.): *Henri Theil's Contributions to Economics and Econometrics.* Vol. I: Econometric Theory and Methodology. 1992 ISBN 0-7923-1548-0

Advanced Studies in Theoretical and Applied Econometrics

24. B. Raj and J. Koerts (eds.): *Henri Theil's Contributions to Economics and Econometrics*. Vol. II: Consumer Demand Analysis and Information Theory. 1992 ISBN 0-7923-1664-9
25. B. Raj and J. Koerts (eds.): *Henri Theil's Contributions to Economics and Econometrics*. Vol. III: Economic Policy and Forecasts, and Management Science. 1992 ISBN 0-7923-1665-7
    Set (23–25) ISBN 0-7923-1666-5
26. P. Fisher: *Rational Expectations in Macroeconomic Models*. 1992 ISBN 0-7923-1903-6
27. L. Phlips and L.D. Taylor (eds.): *Aggregation, Consumption and Trade*. Essays in Honor of H.S. Houthakker. 1992 ISBN 0-7923-2001-8
28. L. Matyas and P. Sevestre (eds.): *The Econometrics of Panel Data*. Handbook of Theory and Applications. 1992 ISBN 0-7923-2043-3
29. S. Selvanathan: *A System-Wide Analysis of International Consumption Patterns*. 1993 ISBN 0-7923-2344-0
30. H. Theil in association with D. Chen, K. Clements and C. Moss: *Studies in Global Econometrics*. 1996 ISBN 0-7923-3660-7
31. P.J. Kehoe and T.J. Kehoe (eds.): *Modeling North American Economic Integration*. 1995 ISBN 0-7923-3751-4
32. C. Wells: *The Kalman Filter in Finance*. 1996 ISBN 0-7923-3771-9
33. L. Matyas and P. Sevestre (eds.): *The Econometrics of Panel Data*. A Handbook of the Theory with Applications Second Revised Edition. 1996 ISBN 0-7923-3787-5
34. B. Assarsson, D. Edgerton, A Hummelmose, I Laurila, K. Rickertson and P.H. Vale: *The Econometrics of Demand Systems*. With Applications to Food Demand in the North Countries. 1996 ISBN 0-7923-4106-6
35. D.A. Griffith, C.G. Amrhein and J-M. Huriot (eds.): *Econometric Advances in Spatial Modelling and Methodology*. Essays in Honour of Jean Paelinck. 1998 ISBN 0-7923-4915-6
36. R.D.H. Heijmans, D.S. G. Pollock and A. Satorra (eds.): *Innovations in Multivariate Statistical Analysis*. 2000 ISBN 0-7923-8636-1
37. R. MacDonald and I. Marsh: *Exchange Rate Modelling*. 2000 ISBN 0-7923-8668-X
38. L. Bauwens and P. Giot: *Econometric Modelling of Stock Market Intraday Activity*. 2001 ISBN 0-7923-7424-X
39. J. Marquez: *Estimating Trade Elasticities*. 2002 ISBN 1-4020-7159-0
40. R. Bhar and S. Hamori: *Hidden Markov Models*. Applications to Financial Economics. 2004 ISBN 1-4020-7899-4
41. P. Tryfos: *The Measurement of Economic Relationships*. 2004 ISBN 1-4020-2616-1
42. M.O. Haque: *Income Elasticity and Economic Development*. Methods and Applications. 2005 ISBN 0-387-24292-9
43. I.F. Razafimahefa and S. Hamori: *International Competitiveness in Africa*. Policy Implications in the Sub-Saharan Region. 2007 ISBN 978-3-540-68920-1

MIX
Papier aus verantwortungsvollen Quellen
Paper from responsible sources
FSC® C105338

If you have any concerns about our products,
you can contact us on
ProductSafety@springernature.com

In case Publisher is established outside the EU,
the EU authorized representative is:
Springer Nature Customer Service Center GmbH
Europaplatz 3, 69115 Heidelberg, Germany

Printed by Libri Plureos GmbH
in Hamburg, Germany